WIFE

MATE, MOTHER, ME!

WIFE

MATE, MOTHER, ME!

Gayle G. Roper

BAKER BOOK HOUSE
Grand Rapids, Michigan

I dedicate this book
with much love
to CHUCK
the perfect husband—for me

Copyright 1975 by
Baker Book House Company

ISBN: 0-8010-7633-1

First printing, September 1976
Second printing, January 1977

Printed in the United States of America

Contents

Chapter 1   The Chief End of a Wife Is . . .
Page 9

Chapter 2   A Wife's Potential—Unlimited
Page 12

Chapter 3   An excellent wife, who can find?
Page 15   For her worth is far above jewels.

Chapter 4   The heart of her husband trusts in her,
Page 18   And he will have no lack of gain.

Chapter 5   She does him good and not evil
Page 22   All the days of her life.

Chapter 6   She looks for wool and flax
Page 25   And works with her hands in delight.

Chapter 7   She is like merchant ships;
Page 29   She brings her food from afar.

Chapter 8   She rises also while it is still night,
Page 32   And gives food to her household,
And portions to her maidens.

Chapter 9   She considers a field and buys it;
Page 38   From her earnings
she plants a vineyard.

Chapter 10   She girds herself with strength
Page 42   And makes her arms strong.

Chapter 11   She senses that her gain is good;
Page 47   Her lamp does not go out at night.

Chapter 12   She stretches out her hands
Page 50   to the distaff,
And her hands grasp the spindle.

Chapter 13   She extends her hand to the poor;
Page 53   And she stretches out her hands
to the needy.

Chapter 14   She is not afraid of the snow
Page 57   for her household,
For all her household are clothed
with scarlet.

Chapter 15   She makes coverings for herself;
Page 61   Her clothing is fine linen and purple.

Chapter 16   Her husband is known in the gates,
Page 64   When he sits among the elders of the land.

Chapter 17   She makes linen garments and sells them,
Page 68   And supplies belts to the tradesmen.

Chapter 18   Strength and dignity are her clothing,
Page 72   And she smiles at the future.

Chapter 19   She opens her mouth in wisdom,
Page 77   And the teaching of kindness
is on her tongue.

Chapter 20   She looks well to the ways
Page 81   of her household,
And does not eat the bread
of idleness.

Chapter 21   Her children rise up and bless her;
Page 86   Her husband also,
and he praises her, saying:
"Many daughters have done nobly,
But you excel them all."

Chapter 22   Charm is deceitful and beauty is vain,
Page 91   But a woman who fears the Lord,
she shall be praised.

Chapter 23   Give her the product of her hands
Page 95   And let her works praise her
in the gates.

Chapter 24   It's a Matter of Balance
Page 98

I

The Chief End of a Wife Is . . .

A few weeks ago my husband Chuck and I had a discussion about me and one of my particularly obvious faults.

"Why can't you be like _____?" Chuck named a friend of ours. "She never has that problem. She manages to handle it. Why can't you?"

"Is that what you want me to be, another her? Okay, that's what I'll be," I said shortly, the very soul of maturity. "I'll be just like her. I'll do the things she does. I'll become another her."

"No," he said with a somewhat frustrated smile. "That's not what I want."

There was a large sigh of relief on my part since that's not what I wanted either. While our friend is a lovely lady, she's not me.

Chuck continued, "Besides, you're more interesting."

I stared at Chuck, smiled, and gave him the biggest hug I could muster. As far as I was concerned he had just given me the ultimate compliment. After twelve years of marriage, I was more interesting. After four moves, two kids, countless nights in curlers, and an extra ten bulgy pounds, I was more interesting. What more can a wife want?

Many people find great pleasure today in knocking marriage. It's restrictive, old-fashioned, and dumb, they say. And it could be argued that these detractors have a point.

Marriage is restrictive. One partner for fifty years definitely limits one's lifestyle. But restriction also brings order and security.

Marriage is old-fashioned. So is love and so is motherhood. But old is not necessarily synonymous with bad.

Marriage can even be classed as dumb, especially on certain days. But it doesn't take a person of much intelligence to see the greater absurdity of throwing matrimony overboard like a piece of sociological flotsam.

Restrictive, old-fashioned, dumb—but interesting! Especially as it should be.

The Westminster Catechism declares that the chief end of man is to glorify God. The chief end of a wife is to be interesting to her husband. And the beauty of it all is that in becoming and remaining interesting to him, you become vital and alive to yourself and a tool of great possibility in the hands of God.

The world is full of how-to-be-a-good-wife books. There are books on reaching his heart through his stomach, on seducing him imaginatively, on decorating his castle, on aiding him in his ventures into the business world, and on supporting him when the world knocks him down. There are books on keeping up with him, and books on slowing him down. There are even books on how to manage after he's gone.

But some of the best advice on wifing was recorded centuries ago. It bears out the thesis that one of the best definitions of a good wife is "interesting."

> *An excellent wife, who can find?*
> *For her worth is far above jewels.*
> *The heart of her husband trusts in her,*
> *And he will have no lack of gain.*
> *She does him good and not evil*
> *All the days of her life.*
> *She looks for wool and flax,*
> *And works with her hands in delight.*
> *She is like merchant ships;*
> *She brings her food from afar.*
> *She rises also while it is still night,*
> *And gives food to her household,*
> *And portions to her maidens.*
> *She considers a field and buys it;*
> *From her earnings she plants a vineyard.*
> *She girds herself with strength,*
> *And makes her arms strong.*
> *She senses that her gain is good;*

Her lamp does not go out at night.
She stretches out her hand to the distaff,
And her hands grasp the spindle.
She extends her hand to the poor;
And she stretches out her hands to the needy.
She is not afraid of the snow for her household,
For all her household are clothed with scarlet.
She makes coverings for herself;
Her clothing is fine linen and purple.
Her husband is known in the gates,
When he sits among the elders of the land.
She makes linen garments and sells them,
And supplies belts to the tradesmen.
Strength and dignity are her clothing,
And she smiles at the future.
She opens her mouth in wisdom,
And the teaching of kindness is on her tongue.
She looks well to the ways of her household,
And does not eat the bread of idleness.
Her children rise up and bless her;
Her husband also, and he praises her, saying:
"Many daughters have done nobly,
But you excel them all."
Charm is deceitful and beauty is vain,
But a woman who fears the Lord, she shall be praised.
Give her the product of her hands,
And let her works praise her in the gates.
                    —Prov. 31:10-31

Isn't this one of the most interesting, captivating, delightful women you've ever met? I think she's great. I invite you to ponder with me her endless qualities—and in so doing I guarantee we'll find many clues to a happy, balanced life for ourselves.

2

A Wife's Potential—Unlimited

It's easy to be intimidated when we read about the fascinating woman of Proverbs, because she's so outstanding. She's got it all together. She has a happy family and a good career. She's organized and content. We'll never make it!

Such negative thinking will guarantee that we'll never make it. Let's go at it positively. If we feel able to develop only one of her characteristics, then we're that much richer, that much more interesting. We can't lose. And besides, there's the unlimited power source of God to mold and change us.

If God left us to ourselves, we could never succeed in our revamping program. Pulling oneself up by one's bootstraps is the classic illustration of the futility of going it alone. How many New Year's resolutions have we broken? How many times have we vowed never to nag our husbands again, never to overeat again, never to spank in anger, never to lose our tempers at our teen-agers, never to bite our nails—the list goes on into infinity.

Failures come and go in our attempts to remold ourselves into more pleasing persons. For some reason, even though we constantly fail, we rarely give up. We psych ourselves up and try again. We might even succeed for a little while, but then we usually slip back. Laziness wins another over perseverance.

That's the way it will be in trying to become like the lady in Proverbs—unless we use God's help.

I have another ideal in my life besides the Biblical woman. It's Jesus Christ. He is very special to me, my Savior and Lord. He was a perfect man; He is God. Yet the Bible tells me to be like Him. ". . . put on the Lord Jesus Christ" (Rom. 13:14). How can I ever put on the attributes and characteristics of Jesus? He was and is perfect. And that I'm not—ask Chuck! It's hard enough just being interesting! There are so many things I do wrong, some unintentionally, some, unhappily, not. The Bible calls this wrong behavior of mine "sin."

"There is none righteous, not even one; there is none who understands, there is none who seeks after God. . . . all have sinned and come short of the glory of God" (Rom. 3:10, 23).

Personally I don't like to admit that I'm a sinner, but I have no choice. I like even less the result of that sin. ". . . through one man sin entered into the world, and death through sin, and so death spread to all men, because all sinned" (Rom. 5:12). Death comes to all because all sin. Death, the universal equalizer. Sin, the universal plague.

But we needn't die spiritually, even though we all have sinned. ". . . the wages of sin is death, but the free gift of God is eternal life in Jesus Christ our Lord" (Rom. 6:23). In Jesus Christ we have eternal life, not death!

Remember the theological term *saved*? This is where it comes in. We're *saved* from sin and death. ". . . God demonstrates His own love toward us, in that while we were yet sinners, Christ died for us" (Rom. 5:8). Christ was our sacrifice to *save* us from sin and death.

So how do we make this salvation a personal thing? "If you confess with your mouth Jesus as Lord, and believe in your heart that God raised Him from the dead, you shall be saved, for with the heart man believes, resulting in righteousness, and with the mouth he confesses, resulting in salvation. For the Scripture says, 'Whoever believes in Him will not be disappointed' " (Rom. 10:9-11).

When we believe, Jesus is not only our ideal, but also our Lord and Savior. We want to please Him and to obey His Word. We want to "put on the Lord Jesus Christ."

When Jesus' death was only one day away and He knew He would be leaving His disciples, He said to them, "And I will ask the Father, and He will give you another Helper, that He may be with you forever. . . . But the Helper, the Holy Spirit, whom the Father will send in My name, He will teach you all things, and bring to your remembrance all that I have said to you" (John 14:16, 26).

Here is where the power to become Christ-like originates, the power to be transformed into the image of God—from the Holy Spirit. Not that we ever achieve total transformation. Sin is still rampant in the world, and the sin nature with which we were born still rears its ugly head. Sanctification, that process of becoming holy, will never be completed until we reach glory.

Still we have within us as Christians the supernatural enabling of the Holy Spirit. As He teaches us and strengthens us, we become more holy, more Christ-like.

What does this have to do with our "excellent wife"? It's the basic power source for the strength to become like her. Part of putting on Christ is becoming the best, most productive person I can be in my circumstances and with my talents.

Without Christ's and the Holy Spirit's power, we might achieve some of the excellent wife's potential, but by their power we can achieve more with greater tranquility.

Accept Christ and take the life-changing power of the Holy Spirit into your life. With prayer, perseverance, and the power of the Holy Spirit, you can be this most interesting woman.

3

An excellent wife, who can find?
For her worth is far above jewels.

Two cows, a packet of gems, a hundred acres of land, a handful of cowrie shells, a billy goat, or a basketful of produce—through the ages all these items have been used by man to buy himself a woman. Every time a marital bargain is struck, the purchaser hopes he's getting a prize worth the price.

Today in our culture, men don't buy their wives. Marital agreements are entered into freely with both parties consenting. But the hope of getting a prize is still there. Even with the high rate of divorce and the open admission of marriage miseries by many, a bride and groom head for the altar confident that their marriage will last, that they will be the one out of ten couples who has an intimate, caring relationship where love deepens, not dies.

The vows are made, the honeymoon taken, and the bride comes home to the difficult business of being a wife.

My sister-in-law Lynn tells of the shock of returning from her honeymoon and suddenly realizing she had to cook dinner.

My mother-in-law recalls coming straight from Niagara Falls to a house peopled with her father-in-law and brother-in-law. The other women of the family were away at a summer home. Mom was expected to cook for all three men.

As she tells it, "You couldn't see the kitchen for the smoke."

My mom admits to adding butter to the bacon when she cooked her first breakfast.

And I remember the hi-fi equipment we got in kit form for wedding presents. Chuck had asked for the kits so he could have the pleasure of building his own stuff. For weeks after the wedding I sat in the living room and watched my new husband in the dining room working on his hi-fi equipment at the rickety table that had cost us $5.00. The look of happiness as he soldered and tinkered, and the look of intense concentration with which he checked his directions were emotions which I had expected would be directed only at me. I'd look soulfully at his oblivious form and mourn my hi-fi widowhood.

Being a wife is never easy, and being an excellent wife is harder yet. A bride is just starting the long, frustrating but richly rewarding task of achieving excellence.

I realize much could be said—and rightly so—about the many lazy, lousy husbands that people our land, but that's not my intent. Proverbs 31:10-31 wasn't written about man. It's written about a woman.

One of the most interesting things about these verses is that they are words of advice given by a mother to her son: "The words of King Lemuel, the oracle which his mother taught him" (Prov. 31:1).

Who King Lemuel was is uncertain. There are no records in the history of Israel of a Lemuel. Some scholars think that Lemuel might actually be another name of Solomon. If so, then the giver of this advice is Bathsheba, wife of David. Actually very little is known of Bathsheba beyond her seduction by David. Even that indicates nothing of her true character, for how does a woman refuse a king?

Whether the advice to the son comes from Bathsheba or the unknown mother of an actual Lemuel is unimportant. The wisdom imparted is what has the great value.

As I see the poor choices countless men and women have made and are making in the selection of their mates, I'm forced to conclude that few mothers share with their daughters *and sons* as Lemuel's mother did. The number of offspring who get decent lectures on the facts of life is small, but the number who get instructions on the innate qualities that make good mates must be smaller yet. And the latter may well be more important than the former. The specifics of sex can be gotten from any comprehensive hygiene book or well-populated street corner. Unfortunately the fine points of making a marriage work are never more perverted than on that same street corner.

It's fascinating to contemplate the fantastic variety of personalities that populate the world. In this multi-faceted throng is the "excellent wife" of each man. That's the beauty of God's creation. One man's excellent wife isn't the same as another's. No two men need exactly the same type of woman. My friend who has the characteristic that Chuck urged me to adopt wouldn't make a good wife for him. I look at former boy friends, fine men with their hearts turned toward Christ, and I know marriage to them would have been disaster. God purposed that I should be Chuck's wife. He knew the compatability of our personalities, and He foresaw the pattern of our growth through the years.

This type of satisfying marriage can come to anyone who has his heart turned toward God. It can come to anyone willing to endure the agony of adapting to another, anyone willing to allow for the give and take of constant companionship. Some are fortunate enough to have God's hand on their marriage from the beginning. Others learn long after the vows are said and the hopes are in shambles about their heads that they must have God in their marriage.

But either way, with the Holy Spirit's power, a good, caring, satisfying, intimate marriage can be built.

4

The heart of her husband trusts in her, And he will have no lack of gain.

"The greatest gift of God is a pious, amiable spouse who fears God, loves his house, and with whom one can live in perfect harmony."—Martin Luther

"A pious, amiable spouse"—certainly an interesting pair of adjectives. The first is God-centered; the second man-centered. A woman who loves God, not in the phony, pompous, self-righteous way we often associate with the word *pious* but with a warm, intense, true affection, is a wife to desire. She will develop love, joy, peace, patience, kindness, goodness, faithfulness, gentleness, and self-control (Gal. 5:22-3). Such a woman will automatically be amiable, pleasant to live with, a wife in which the heart of a husband can trust.

Notice that this isn't just expecting a wife to be faithful in sex. It's much more encompassing than that.

How thoroughly can your husband trust you? Can he have confidence in how you will react to a given set of circumstances? Does he know what to expect from you? Can he foresee your response to problems and pleasantries? Not that any person could ever—maybe even should ever—know someone completely. But basically we do follow patterns.

There are women so touchy that their husbands withhold information rather than face the expected explosion. The screamers would just storm and shout; the whiners would just mope and complain.

Not so our Proverbs lady. The heart of her husband could trust her. He foresaw a favorable response, a helpful manner, an uncritical attitude. What a challenge in the nitty-gritty of living.

"Judy, I won't be able to make it home for dinner tonight. This sales meeting will last a couple more hours."

"I hate to have to tell you this just after you've gotten settled in, Sally, but I've been transferred again."

"Mr. and Mrs. Andrews, I'm sorry to have to tell you this, but your son has cystic fibrosis. The prognosis isn't good."

"Molly, I just got laid off. No warning, no nothing."

Situations similar to these develop in all our lives from time to time. Can the hearts of our husbands depend on us to take disappointments and difficulties in stride? Or are we among the many wives whose husbands can count on us to get hysterical, belligerent, argumentative, withdrawn, or critical?

Living positively with unhappy situations does not come automatically. It's all too easy for the unlovely side of ourselves to surface when things burden us. Only close fellowship with the Lord can give us the ability to respond in the proper way. We learn to put off the old man and his unhealthy, hurtful attitudes and put on the new man with his positive, loving manner.

The experience of our friends Bob and Linda demonstrates how we can take a very undesirable circumstance and let it be a tool to fashion us into the Christ-like people the Lord wants us to be.

It was just after New Year's Day that Bob unexpectedly lost his job. He went to work as usual, and he was home an hour later, unemployed. With the uncertainty of today's job market, there was real cause for concern. The key to the issue was keeping the concern in proportion.

From the beginning Bob and Linda gave the problem to the Lord. They accepted Bob's unemployment as part of God's plan for them at that time. They prayed about it privately and publicly, admitting the problem but never moaning about it.

Linda is a clever, dynamic, aggressive, humorous, thoroughly enjoyable young woman. Bob says she's so busy planning all the time that he gets tired just listening. Being patient is not Linda's strong point. She describes herself as "hyper." She's efficient, organized, and likes to do things *now*.

As a result, the waiting for a new job was extremely difficult for her, especially since she couldn't *do* anything about it herself.

From the beginning Linda determined that with the Lord's help, she would be a supportive wife, not a nag. She would voice her opinions on a job possibility or interview once or twice; then she would bite her tongue. For Linda that was restraint with a capital R.

When Bob lost his job, they had just bought a new house which had cleaned out their savings. They did have $1000 in the bank, but that was earmarked to pay for the adoption of their second Korean child. They began praying that the Lord would protect the baby's money. If they had to touch it, who knew when they would ever be able to replace it? It was bad enough having to tell the social worker about Bob's unemployment and halt the adoption apparatus temporarily.

God honored their prayers (and their over-all attitude) and sent a series of mini-miracles to bless and strengthen them.

First there was a $25.00 check from friends who had just gone through the same jobless situation and who were hardly back on their own financial feet.

Then there was a care package from the pastor and his wife containing meat and canned goods.

Linda's father offered them $20.00 a week for groceries for the duration. Bob's mother bought them a tank of gas every time they came for a meal. Friends invited them for dinner.

An estate that Bob was executor for was settled, releasing the money they had hoped to have for Christmas but which the Lord knew they would need later.

Linda's sister-in-law Jesse and her brother Phil, a seminarian, twice gave Bob and Linda money that Phil had to work overtime to earn.

A friend bought two weeks' worth of meat for them. Another gave Linda some material that she stretched into a spring outfit for herself and a suit for two-year-old Scott.

A concerned woman at church came up to Bob one Sunday morning after the service and handed him a hefty check.

"The Lord told me to give this to you."

When Linda went for her yearly gynecological check-up, the doctor said that he could tell that she and Bob must be taking the situation with the proper attitude because her body showed no signs of stress. He then refused to bill her for the check-up.

When it looked like they might need to touch the baby's money for the mortgage payment, the Lord intervened again. Bob's income tax refund arrived.

Of his unemployment, Bob says that on the whole it was a positive experience. He *knew* the Lord was in it. He learned to depend on people more, to receive graciously. It forced him into alternative moves, like away from the deadend job he had. And it was thrilling to see the Lord work in such a practical way.

"We've needed His strength before," says Bob. "When we learned we couldn't have children, we hung onto Him then. But this was a different type of supplying, and it was exciting."

Behind Bob and his ability to cope so well with his unpleasant predicament was his partner Linda. His heart could trust her. She built him up. She helped him practically by working hard at budget stretching. She helped him emotionally by encouraging, not criticizing. She helped him spiritually by praying for him and with him.

No hysterics, no insecurity. Just waiting on the Lord for His time and leading. Just casting all their cares on Him and leaving them there. When the job of God's choice finally appeared, they gratefully accepted it, richer for having been poor, more deeply married for having to suffer together.

Being a woman your husband can depend on is one of the difficult jobs of wifing. It requires constant effort, but it reaps great rewards in appreciation and love.

5

She does him good and not evil
All the days of her life.

No woman goes into marriage with the avowed purpose of doing her man evil. It would be sheer folly to plan to hinder the one with whom her destiny is so closely entwined.

That doesn't mean that doing him good comes automatically or easily. Far from it. Helping him, supporting him, uplifting him, and comforting him are hard work.

Perhaps one of the reasons we often fail to do him the good we intend is because we are confused about our roles. What is a wife? Who is a wife? How can she know what's best for her husband?

The definitive passage on a Christian marriage is found in Ephesians 5:22ff:

> Wives, be subject to your own husbands, as to the Lord. For the husband is the head of the wife, as Christ also is the head of the church, He Himself being the Savior of the body. But as the church is subject to Christ, so also the wives ought to be to their husbands in everything. Husbands, love your wives, just as Christ also loved the church and gave Himself up for her; . . . So husbands ought also to love their own wives as their own bodies. He who loves his own wife loves himself; for no one ever hateth his own flesh, but nourishes and cherishes it, just as Christ also does the church, because we are members of His body. For this cause a man shall leave his father and mother, and shall cleave to his wife; and the two shall become one flesh.

These are heady words, but in them lies the key to marital success.

"The heart of these words to husbands and to the wives can be reached quickly by asking two questions: Husbands, do you love your wives enough to die for them? Wives, do you love your husbands enough to live for them?" (Jay E. Adams, *Christian Living in the Home*, Baker, 1972, p.70)

It has been said that dying for a cause is easier than living for it. I don't know. If so, then we women may have the harder part of the marriage bargain, for we must do the living for the cause of a happy home and husband.

To many women, the idea of being submissive sounds degrading. In an era when women have decided quite rightly not to be content with unequal social and professional status, willing subjection to a husband sounds reactionary, unfair, anachronistic. If it weren't that the injunction were Scriptural, I'd be unwilling to defend it myself. But it is Biblical. I must be willing to accept it, or I'm undercutting the authority of God's Word.

There is logic, both practical and theological, behind the concept of subjection.

There is the practical argument that there must be final authority in every organization. Otherwise there's anarchy. Marriage is a cooperative venture, but it isn't a democratic one.

Theologically—and to a Christian woman, these arguments should be of prime importance—there are two reasons for the concept of the wife's submission. First, there is creation. Adam came first. Why God saw fit to create Adam first, I don't know. But He did. Eve came second, and she was the helpmeet.

Secondly, there is the Fall. Eve took of the fruit before her husband, and part of her punishment from God was that her husband should rule over her (Gen. 3:16).

There is yet another reason for following the Biblical principle of headship. *It works.* Time after time in marriage after marriage, letting the husband assume his position as leader has worked.

Please understand that being subject to Chuck doesn't make me less of a person. I don't give up my right to think or to be an individual when I yield my fight for marital equality. I don't even give up my right to disagree. Ephesians 5 doesn't say I have to be an emotional dishrag. Our friend in Proverbs certainly wasn't a rubber stamp.

23

I admit that I have had times of rebellion against this submission concept. I'm an achiever by nature, and I don't like being second in anything. I feel that I'm no less capable than a man. Why should I have to be the submissive one?

Because the Bible tells me I must be. And here lies the key to the whole issue. Before I'm willing to be subject to my husband, I must be willing to be submissive to my Lord. Only when Jesus Christ and I are in proper relationship and the Holy Spirit controls my life am I willing to obey His Word. Only as I bow before Him am I willing to bow before my husband with grace and love.

Being willing to obey does restrict me, but it doesn't dilute me. It merely gives a basic, needed structure to my marriage relationship.

We are doing our husbands the greatest good we can when we allow them to be the head of their homes. It's no easy job for them. As Jay Adams whimsically puts it, "As manager, your husband bears many fearful responsibilities. Perhaps the most perplexing and difficult of all his responsibilities is managing you! Think about it for a while. If you think it's a difficult job to submit, think about his job. He must manage you" (op. cit., p.83).

According to Scripture, marriage is for keeps. We are to do our husbands good *all the days of our lives*. Divorce is only for the most extreme of circumstances.

I am concerned for my sons as they grow up in a culture where multiple marriage is so common. Teaching them to exercise great care and much prayer in the selection of their wives is high on my list of priorities. I pray now for these girls, whoever they are, wherever they are, because only God can prepare them for my sons. It's not that I'm pushy and feel my sons must marry. That will be their option. It's that prayer and care before the fact can save much heartache after. It's preventive prayer rather than corrective.

6

She looks for wool and flax
And works with her hands in delight.

It's more than a small sign of changing times when the lady of one era takes wool and flax and makes cloth, while the lady of a later era (me) wouldn't know where to find flax or what to do with flax or wool if they were given me.

Obviously this passage is meant to be more than a lesson in linen-making. And it certainly is.

Did you notice how the woman *looked* for her materials? She didn't sit around and wait for Ben Eli, the tailor, to bring her the finished product, or for Abigail across the street to shame her into action. Our lady *sought* what she needed.

We would do well to follow her example whether our need is for material supplies as hers was or for emotional or spiritual help. When the solution to a particularly knotty problem is elusive, it's too easy to let the difficulty ride. We hope that if we ignore it, ostrich-like, it'll go away.

But that's not what our lady teaches us. If we have a burden, we must look for the best way to lift it.

Our pastor does much counseling of people with life-crushing needs. One question he always asks new counselees is, "What have you done about your problem before now?" The answer, almost without fail, is, "Pray."

Prayer is wonderful. There's no argument there. Prayer is the means of laying our problems before God and asking for His help. As His children, this is our privilege. But prayer is only part of the solution.

Rarely does God hand out miracles like a magician saying, "Presto!", and pulling a rabbit from a hat. What would we learn from such painless cures? Nothing.

God wants us to lay our problems at His feet, to trust Him to help us, and then to *seek* for His answers.

Our friends Pauline and Martin had trouble with their teenage children. Being Christians, they prayed much about it. They read their Bibles and found some basic guidelines for the family. They wanted to implement them in their home, but being quiet and reticent by nature, they had a hard time facing the onslaught of the war for adolescent independence. What should they do? What did the Lord expect of them? Should they force Sunday school on their three kids who were determined to go no nearer church than their warm beds each Sunday morning?

Pauline and Martin were desperate. So they sought help. They went to a Christian man well trained in family counseling. He taught them practical methods of coping, new workable ideas of putting the Biblical principles to work. In time the troubled family was healed.

Had the help not been sought, the trouble would have continued to fester until there was deep anger on the kids' part not only toward Pauline and Martin, but also toward God.

We don't all have trained counselors conveniently handy. But there are alternatives. There are pastors, friends mature in their faith, or some of the excellent recent Christian books. God doesn't teach us all through the same avenues.

But one promise I can make. His help is always there if we come seeking with a heart that's willing to follow. God has a wonderful way of providing for His people. "I will instruct you and teach you in the way which you should go; I will counsel you with My eye upon you" (Ps. 32:8).

Be prepared. The major outcome of seeking His help may be an inner revolution. As we pray and seek, the Lord may change our own ideas and desires. This is no less a miracle than manna in the wilderness, especially as we consider how stubborn and self-willed we are.

One of the things most guaranteed to send my sons into fits is a request to pick up their toys. Absolute despair sets in. Wails of persecution mingle with the sounds of breast-beating as they protest the completely brutal treatment of a mother who would ask such lovely and talented children to work. Child Labor Laws were passed to protect youngsters from just such ogres as I.

There are jobs required of wives and mothers that are as

unlovely to us as picking up toys is to my guys. We can go about these unending drudge jobs with the spirit of a child or the mature willingness of our winsome woman. She worked "in delight," and I'm sure spinning flax couldn't have won any awards for mental stimulation.

Have you noticed as you go into various homes and offices that there are places that you enjoy more than others? If you've bothered to analyze why, it's probably based on the subtle atmosphere created by the people who reside or work there. A happy, smiling face sets the tone for a pleasant atmosphere. A drawn, grim face squelches even the brilliance of the sunshine.

A woman who would be pleasant company must be a willing worker. As soon as she lowers herself to complaining and grousing, she is no longer a joy to be with. We all have enough concerns of our own and find no pleasure in listening to the foolish ramblings of an unhappy woman.

No one expects us to like everything we have to do, like dusting, washing the dishes, matching up socks, or typing endless lists for a crotchety boss. But, Christian woman, God expects us to do these things willingly. "Whatever your hand finds to do, verily, do it with all your might" (Eccles. 9:10). "And whatever you do in word or deed, do all in the name of the Lord Jesus, giving thanks through Him to God the Father" (Col. 3:17).

Perhaps the hardest place to work willingly and with delight is in our own home. As soon as we finish a job, a husband, child, or pet immediately undoes it. It's highly frustrating.

And the work is generally done alone. Even the dreariest of chores would be lightened if we only had someone with whom to share them. But as we iron, make beds, wash endless mountains of soiled clothes, and sweep, we have only ourselves to converse with—unless we've fostered such a close friendship with the Lord that we can use that time to talk with Him.

I think it falls to the woman to set the tone of a home. If she is quick-tempered and caustic and looses control at the slightest ripple in the smooth surface of her life, her family will also have a low threshold of control. If she sasses her husband and kids, they will sass her right back. No one will have any more restraint than a flare set to a match.

However, if the woman of the household is pleasant, consistent, and God-oriented, she can pass these positive traits on to her family, too. The catch is that these positive traits, these fruit of the Spirit listed in Galatians 5:22-3, require constant vigilance. Not only are our families out to inadvertently trip us up, but Satan is actively trying to make us stumble. Only constant, daily communion with Christ can help us beat our enemies, foreign and domestic.

7

She is like merchant ships;
She brings her food from afar.

There is something uncomfortable about being compared to a ship. Visions of old tubs come to mind, and there is the secret fear that this is the image being conveyed.

Even if the physical simile is less than flattering, the concept being presented is good. It pictures a wife who shops widely and well for her family. She is a menu planner who selects the components of each given meal carefully. Green vegetables, meats, fruit, milk—all good foods are provided. She also shops at the outlets, saving a fortune on clothes. She passes on to others the kids' clothing as it gets outgrown.

This doesn't mean that she has to be a home economics expert. She just uses well the basic knowledge she has diligently acquired.

Many women, myself included, have a love-hate relationship with shopping and cooking.

At times and in the right mood, it can be a real joy to create a culinary masterpiece. The first time I ever made a quiche Lorraine I had a wonderful time. And I love shopping and cooking for company, even if my entertaining isn't always book perfect. One evening my baked stuffed potatoes exploded all over the oven, sending out waves of that characteristic scorching smell. After everyone came out to the kitchen to view the wreckage, I managed to scrape together enough smashed mashed to give each of the six men about a tablespoon-size serving. Thankfully I had plenty of rolls.

But there are times when my kitchen becomes a trap that threatens to imprison me for life. My cellmates are dirty dishes and garbage. My life's work is reduced to one long KP assignment. Dinner time draws near and I reach in panic for *1001 Ways to Cook With Ground Beef*, and nothing looks good.

It's in the unhappy times, the I-never-felt-less-like-a-merchant-ship times, that we play the dangerous *If Only* game.

"If only I had married a millionaire."

"If only I could get out of this kitchen trap and never return."

"If only I had a maid."

"If only my husband would help me."

Not that these *if only's* are wrong in themselves. It's the frame of mind they create. They breed discouragement, dissatisfaction, and frustration.

If you married a millionaire, great. If you can afford a maid, great. If your husband will help (without nagging), great. But if not, and that's most of us, don't waste your time playing *If Only*. You are guaranteed to lose. Dreaming is wonderful, but don't waste your life on it.

There's an interesting thing about people addicted to playing *If Only*. They rarely accomplish anything. Whether it's a businessman who never advances because he's too busy being unhappy to be creative or the homemaker who complains constantly about her lot in life—which, incidentally, she chose—the principle is the same. *If Only* drains joy the way an illness saps energy.

As we mope around playing our hopeless game, we miss countless opportunities to lift our lives out of the mundane track everyone seems to follow. We expend all our energies negatively instead of thinking positively, creatively.

Next time there's a temptation to play *If Only*, plan a picnic in the living room before the fireplace or a breakfast on the back porch. Instead of wasting energy grousing while the hamburgers fry, make personalized place cards for each family member with words of love and appreciation inside. My favorite way of lifting the afternoon drudges is Edith Schaeffer's delightful idea of Treasure Hunt Meals (*Hidden Art*, Wheaton, Tyndale, 1971).

The gist of this plan is to make up various clues, each leading to the next. After ten or so clues leading the kids and Dad, if he's cooperative or the kids can't read, all over the house, the appetizer is discovered. Peanut butter crackers or cheese hunks or a grapefruit half—anything will do. On occasion we've found appetizers in Jeff's toy chest and Chip's closet. We ate them on the spot.

More clues lead to the next course. Once we ate the dinner itself in our bedroom. I sent the kids and Chuck downstairs for the last clue. While they were gone, I set up the card table and chairs I had previously stashed under our bed. I ran the casserole and tableware in from the kitchen just in time to beat my men. After dinner, off they went in search of dessert. It was a wonderful family time, and the kids loved it.

Being a merchant ship plowing swiftly and gracefully through the seas of our special lives is hard work. But the positive results to ourselves and our family make all the harrowing fights with and defeats of the shoals of *If Only* well worth the effort.

8

**She rises also while it is still night,
And gives food to her household,
And portions to her maidens.**

There are few things in this life harder to take than an early riser who delights in getting up with the sun. Inevitably these people awake with a song, whistling their way through their morning shower, and eating big breakfasts. They are even ready for their morning appointments early, arriving bright-eyed while the rest of humanity looks at them askance through eyes still heavy with sleep.

To be a parent blessed with such a child is a trial almost beyond endurance. When a cheery little voice awakens morning after morning at 5:30 or 6, first singing to you from his crib, then growing up to pad in and, five inches from your ear, happily urges you to get up, it calls for the most stoic of parents and the most fervent of prayers.

The almost universal desire to sleep in is a particularly subtle trap to which a housewife is especially susceptible. At first it's just a few minutes more, then a few more. Soon getting up to fix breakfast becomes too much. The kids and your husband are big enough to pour their own Cheerios and corn flakes. Before you realize it, everyone is gone for the day before you even rise.

Sharing yourself with your family at breakfast is important. That doesn't mean that you have to force yourself to be cheery and chattery. It means you should just be there.

Sending the kids off to school with a smile is an expression of love. They will see enough that is unlovely before they return to you. Let them at least begin the day with the knowledge that you care. And don't just push them out the door. Watch them out of sight. Let them know in this subtle way that you care. They will usually not turn to acknowledge your presence at the door, but on those few days when they need extra reassurance, a quick glance at your smile will help them.

My parents still watch us off every time we visit. It's satisfying to know they still care.

A husband needs this daily send-off, too. Don't just let him disappear automatically. That's a sign of apathy, and marriage is no place for that deadener of emotions.

Unless it's a case where ill health dictates a longer than usual rest, most women who sleep in do it for one of two reasons: lazinesss or boredom.

Laziness wasn't a problem for our lady in Proverbs. She is the picture of busyness in the good sense. That doesn't mean that she wasn't tempted to give up occasionally. That doesn't mean that she didn't feel like pulling the wool she was spinning up over her weary eyes and ignoring everybody and everything for a while. It does mean that she was mature enough not to give in.

The companion of laziness, boredom, is a real problem with many women. It's been said that the most discontented people are women graduates of a liberal arts college who have to stay home with small children. They wake up each morning and the day stretches barren before them. What will they do with the next sixteen hours? Shop? Wash clothes? Blow noses? Make beds? Do dishes? Change diapers? They did that all day yesterday! Why bother to get up?

If that's the sum total of your life, I don't think I'd want to get up either. If that's the extent of your existence, it's time for a change. There are so many possibilities if you've got the initiative to go searching by prayer for your personal answer.

Remember that the power of the Holy Spirit is available to you to provide the abundant life that Jesus promised in John 10:10. That fulfilled life isn't some magical state of mind achieved by a few super-spiritual people. It's a life of Christ-oriented action. Satan achieves a fantastic victory if he keeps us bored and listless. Women with purpose, women with Christ-centered goals, women working out their salvation, proving their salvation by their actions are a powerful force. They are alive, vital, and far from bored.

Pray about your boredom.

"God, dear Father, I'm bored! I love my home, my kids, but I'm bored! What can I do? Give me an answer, You who promised to meet all my needs. Thank You."

Remember how submission to our husbands was only possible after submission to the Lord? Well, escape from boredom is guaranteed only by the same path. If Christ has your life, He will fill it with interesting things, have no fear. He will also teach you to like your responsibilities more. (That's not what you want? You want release from them? Never expect the Lord to provide that. The Christian life is one of Christ-centered self-discipline, not escape.)

Let me make a suggestion for a sure cure to boredom. Ask some of your neighbors, Christian and non-Christian, over one morning a week or every other week to study the Bible together. Don't just discuss what Mary, Myra, and Myrna think. Get into the Bible itself. There are many good Bible study courses with nice thick teacher's manuals to help you out. If teaching isn't your gift, invite someone else to teach in your home. Or volunteer to be a babysitter at a Bible study.

I was first involved in such a study when I was in college. When I look back now at how ignorant I was, it's a true miracle that anything was ever accomplished. In my present Bible study group we have ten women of many backgrounds. We've been together for over two years now, and we truly love each other in the Lord. Our times of study and prayer together have enriched us all.

We meet for two hours every other Tuesday morning. For an hour we chat, have coffee and breakfast cake, share the happenings of the two weeks since we've been together. Then we have a prayer time. We pray out loud, conversationally. If someone feels uncomfortable praying out loud, she will just say, "Let's pray for so-and-so." And we'll all pray silently for that request. Then we exchange names of prayer partners for the next two weeks. This praying daily for one specific girl has drawn us closer to each other. We also exchange any good Christian books we've read recently. There are a number of excellent Christian books on the market today. We finish with our study time, using a workbook study so that we all do preparation before we come and have something to contribute. The Lord has taught us each things that we personally needed to learn.

Another possibility—how many non-Christian women do you know? Many Christian homemakers know almost none. How sad this must make the Lord who asked us to share His Gospel with the world. So go find some women. Join some civic organization whose purpose you can support. Go to the Y for exercise classes. Volunteer to serve on the PTA board. In a little while you'll get to know some new people, and there's your mission field. One sure cure for boredom is to be involved in sharing Him.

Other helps for boredom might include taking a correspondence course in some field that intrigues you. Or you might volunteer to visit your church's shut-ins or the old folks' home down the block. It may not be lovely, but it's necessary. If you do visit older people, take your young children with you. Little people give great pleasure to elderly people, like sunbeams on a cloudy day.

It doesn't matter so much what you do just as long as you do. To waste life being bored is worse than wasting it playing If Only. At least if only-ers are thinking.

Even with all the positive motivation of conquering your world for Christ, breaking the habit of sleeping in can be a real trauma. I know; I've been through it. For years I would get up, give Chuck and the boys their breakfasts, see Chuck off, and while the boys watched Captain Kangaroo and Sesame Street, I'd crawl back in bed. It was so great!

But I finally realized that I was not only creating practical problems for myself (like not being sleepy at night) but I was also wasting irreplaceable time for which I would be held accountable later.

I read somewhere about praising God for each day first thing on waking. Thank Him for the blessings and challenges this day will bring to you. I decided to try it. Each morning when it was time to get up, I prayed, "Thank you, Lord, for another morning. Thank you for today. Help me use it wisely."

I found I couldn't honestly be thankful for another day of life and still want to waste it sleeping in.

The reference to our woman in Proverbs having maids (plural, no less) makes me feel like saying, "I'll take half a dozen, please." Not being a fan of housework, I would be very happy to have someone take care of it all for me. And I think that if anyone can afford such service, fine. The only catch is that the free time thus acquired had better be used positively for the Lord.

Most of us however are far from the maids category. But that doesn't mean that we don't yearn to be freed, at least temporarily, from the relentless responsibilities that pursue us. Everyone, and especially the housebound homemaker, needs some time alone, some time to strengthen the inner being. I firmly feel that a woman does herself, her family, and ultimately her Lord a disservice if she doesn't find some time daily to do not what is wanted of her, but what she wants to do.

For mothers with young children, this may be nap time. Don't waste all that beautiful quietness on housework. Use it to relax, to develop your mind and expand your horizons. Use it to read good books, develop a hobby, write letters or a book, listen to music. Use it as your quiet time with the Lord. But use it and use it well.

For the mother of small children, there's also the possibility of acquiring free time by exchanging baby sitting time with a friend or two.

"I'll watch your Bobby on Tuesday if you'll watch my Billy on Thursday."

When the kids get older and are off to school all day, the time alone can be lost in car pools, meetings, or squandered on the wasteland of daytime TV, if you're not careful. Choose your activities so that there's still that private time to grow as an individual.

A woman working a full-time job has the same need for time alone, time not given to her family or her boss. Finding this time calls for tremendous effort, but it may be what saves her from emotional collapse.

I found one inexpensive way to get out alone, and I used it for years. Every other week on my shopping night, I prepared dinner for Chuck and the boys as usual. Then as Chuck came in, I went out. I'd drive to a nearby drug store or diner and order a hamburger and Coke for my dinner. Beef Wellington could never taste better than those meals in freedom. I'd prop a book against the napkin holder and read as I ate. It was a release to be alone and responsible to no one. Then I'd go shopping at my leisure and return to my three guys refreshed.

Real live maids may be impossible, but a little imagination may well supply the needed free time for relaxation and growth.

9

She considers a field and buys it; From her earnings she plants a vineyard.

Today women are achieving in fields of endeavor they couldn't even enter a few years ago. Women doctors are no longer curiosities. Women lawyers aren't considered sure losers. We have mailpersons, salespersons, and telephone line-persons. Probably somewhere there is even a doorperson.

This great expansion of the job horizon for women is good. For years capable women were discounted simply because they were women. Sadly by some people and in some places women are still ignored or belittled. I know of a Christian business firm that, when money is tight, will hire a woman for the job and automatically pay her less. Disgusting.

In their righteous anger at being so mistreated, women have attacked the Bible along with the male chauvinists as perpetuating the old class order where women were less than people.

But that oft-heard criticism of God's Word isn't justified. For years the world, including Christendom, has taken the Biblical standards for the home and church—which are male led—and applied them incorrectly to society and the job market. The Bible doesn't do that. God's Word allows a woman to achieve apart from the home and church as much as she wants or is able. No where does Scripture say "A woman shall not work." No where does Scripture say that a woman must submit to all men and therefore never be the manager or director of men in a working situation. The only man the Bible says a woman must submit to is her own husband. In the world of business, there are no strictures on a woman except her own abilities and initiative.

In Genesis 1:26-28, when God created man and woman, He gave them dominion over His creation. "Then God said, 'Let Us make man in Our image, according to Our likeness; and let them rule over the fish of the sea and the birds of the sky and over the cattle and over the all the earth, and over every creeping thing that creeps on the earth.' And God created man in His own image, in the image of God created He him; male and female He created them. And God blessed them; and God said to them, 'Be fruitful and multiply and fill the earth, and subdue it; and rule over the fish of the sea and over the birds of the sky, and over every living thing that moves on the earth.' "

The woman Eve worked beside her man.

In Ruth 2 we read, "And Ruth the Moabitess said to Naomi, 'Please let me go to the field and glean among the ears of grain after one in whose sight I may find favor.' And she said to her, 'Go, my daughter.' So she departed and went and gleaned in the fields after the reapers" (vs.2, 3a).

Ruth, the Gentile from whose line the Lord descended, worked. She wasn't paid a salary, but she earned her living. And she wasn't degraded by this labor, for Boaz, a man of position, married her after he met her working in his fields.

Our lady in Proverbs, a woman of means as denoted by her having maids, worked. She bought a field and planted it with the vines she had purchased from her own money. She made clothes and belts and sold them to the merchants (31:24).

In the New Testament there is Lydia of Philippi, Paul's first European convert (Acts 16:14-15). She was a businesswoman, a seller of purple fabrics. Never does Paul, supposedly an enemy of women, criticize Lydia for pursuing her occupation. In fact Paul gives tacit approval to her working when he and his party come and stay with her, enjoying one of the financial rewards of her working—prosperity great enough to entertain a group of people for a prolonged period of time.

Priscilla and Aquilla were other friends of Paul with whom he stayed, this time in Corinth (Acts 18:1-3). This married couple was engaged in the same trade as Paul, tentmaking. ". . . They (Priscilla and Aquilla) were working, for by trade they were tentmakers." Again there is no indication of Paul's being unhappy with Priscilla's commercial enterprise. In fact Paul thinks highly enough of Priscilla to name her with her husband as receiving his special greeting in Romans 16:3 and I Corinthians 16:19.

Many people feel that if there is no other financial recourse for a woman, then she should work. If, like Ruth, it's work or starve, then definitely she should work. However, if a woman doesn't have to work, then she shouldn't.

I disagree. If it's acceptable for a woman to work only when there is financial need, that's practicing a subtle form of situation ethics. Either any woman may work or she may not.

Now let me qualify my statement.

For a single girl there is one condition placed on her work. She must seek out and do the work that God has for her, and she must do her best in it. (Of course, all persons employed, male or female, are enjoined to serve their employers well in Ephesians 6:5, 6.)

A married woman has another proviso to consider. "Wives, be subject to your own husbands."

It would be foolish to think that postmarriage plans can be made as independently as premarriage ones. The combining of two lives into one automatically brings the principles of Ephesians 5 into play. Should the church go off making decisions without consulting the Lord? No more should the wife without consulting the husband.

So, if as a married woman you choose to work, it may only be with the consent of your husband.

He won't agree and you're going mad with boredom?

The trite, tired, old saying, "Prayer changes things" is trite and tired because it's said over and over. And it's said over and over because it's true. Prayer does change things.

As you pray that the Lord will move your Matt from his bull-headed, bigoted, old-fashioned notion that wives shouldn't work, be certain to also pray for the grace to submit to Matt's headship, even though you feel his domination is unfair.

Perhaps he fights so hard to be master because your fight for freedom scares him. Let him be lord of the manor. Let him be secure in what he feels—and what the Bible teaches—are his areas of authority. When he's no longer scared of losing his position, he'll be much more flexible.

Too, you might be certain that Matt has a chance to meet and converse with other Christian men whose wives work. Let him see that their marriages run smoothly, perhaps more so, because the women are happy and fulfilled.

Maybe it will become prudent for you to suggest a compromise. A part-time job may give you your outlet and relieve his fears of the house falling down about his ears.

I didn't begin writing at the lovely, office-sized desk at which I'm writing now. Nor did I begin with the wonderful electric typewriter that Chuck got me for my last birthday. I began typing with two fingers on an old portable left over from college days as I was seated at the kitchen table. It's taken me six years to move up to this desk, this typewriter, and four fingers.

It's important to recognize that if your Matt is like most men, the situation won't change overnight. Nor should it. The position of working wife is too demanding to be entered into lightly.

IO

She girds herself with strength
And makes her arms strong.

As I write this, I'm sitting in my backyard in the sun. My five-year-old, Jeff, is busy on the swing set, apparently trying to prove that there really is a link between man and monkey, or at least boy and monkey. He climbs, he swings, he scrambles, and occasionally he yells, "Look, Mom, I can do this good!"

All youngsters enjoy physical activity. They run, jump, climb, and play with great abandon, girls as well as boys. We're in the climbing stage around here. Chuck has decided that if one of the guys wants to climb a tree, it's all right. But either he or I should be nearby watching. I've told him I can't follow his reasoning. First, it's torture to watch them go up so high. Second, if they should happen to fall, I'd never be able to prevent it. So why torment myself for no reason? I can hear the screams whether I look or not, and if it's not, I save myself shattered nerves.

But kids do need exercise of all kinds to help their bodies develop.

Unfortunately, somewhere in their early teens, girls often decide that physical exertion is unladylike. By the time they marry, they ride everywhere, complain bitterly if an elevator is broken, and do as little as possible that might make them sweat.

By the time these girls reach their thirties, their bodies are so out of shape it's a shame. I don't mean that figures are necessarily gone. I mean that the body itself has become soft, the muscles weak.

Our lady in Proverbs kept herself physically conditioned. She kept her muscles toned, her lungs breathing, deeply. She girded herself with strength. She undoubtedly understood that her body was a gift from God to be treated with care.

How many hours and dollars we American women spend on making our bodies *look* good. We keep thousands of beauticians employed, purchase makeup to do every conceivable thing to our faces, and buy clothes until our closets won't hold any more.

The problem is that while we spend all this time and energy on our appearance we spend very little on the upkeep of the body itself. We don't eat properly. We don't exercise enough.

Mere outer appearance isn't that important in total physical health, for the obvious, visual you doesn't count nearly as much as the inner, conditioned you.

There is such a beautiful parallel to our spiritual beings here. The inner man is most important physically and spiritually, for only as the basic person is healthy can the rest of the person be truly strong.

Good works may cover a multitude of sins, but in the end, the inner corruption will bring you down. Makeup and clothes may cover a poorly conditioned body, but in time the anatomical weaknesses will kill.

Just as our spiritual man requires constant care, so does our physical. As one requires self-discipline and denial, so does the other. As the rewards of one are worth the sacrifice, so are the pleasures of the other.

If you are like me, exercising to control the physical inner man is a difficult thing. Deep-knee bends and situps leave something to be desired in the way of sought after activities. I greatly admire those who can keep up a regimen of these exercises, whether alone at home or in a class at the Y.

I seem to have found my personal answer to the need for exercise in walking. We live semi-country, and the local reservoir is just down the road. I've begun walking around it at least five times a week. Once around takes me about forty-five minutes, but I can do a lot of thinking, or even carry a book along and read as I walk.

Somedays it takes finagling of schedules to get me loose from the house. I can't go during the day because of the boys. In the winter when it gets dark early, I go as soon as Chuck gets home, and we eat later. In the summer, the problem of when is less acute because of the longer daylight. Next year both boys will be gone every day, and I'll be able to walk while they're in school.

Teaching myself discipline in the area of foods is another

43

difficult job. There was a day when I could eat anything. No more. So I'm working and praying and learning. I eat on a smaller plate. I buy cookies I don't like. I shop on a full stomach. And I give my snacks to the Lord. This last one is a hard one.

"Lord, I know I shouldn't have this soda and cookies, so I give them to you."

Then I get busy quickly to remove myself from the temptation.

Sometimes I forget quite honestly and am halfway through a snack before I realize it. Other times I say in effect, "Phooey, Lord. I'm really hungry tonight. You understand, right?"

And He does, all too well. He understands my weakness and lack of self-control. He loves me anyway.

Since we are responsible before God for caring for our bodies which Paul calls temples of the Holy Spirit, it should be obvious that preventive medicine is also a must. Yearly physicals with breast examinations and Pap tests should be routine for every woman.

But there are some diseases that are beyond our control. When one of these unforeseen and uncontrollable illnesses strike, it's how we handle it that makes all the difference in our Christian experience. If we take our illness and give it to the Lord, He'll bless us even in the midst of the pain and distress.

When such a situation strikes us, we are not necessarily terrible Christians if we react with anger. Anger is a natural response to something we don't like. We must be certain, however, that we don't nurse the anger and cling to it.

"God, did you really have to give me this? I was quite content without it! In fact, I don't want it! It scares me. But, God, I realize I have to trust Your wisdom. I don't understand. I don't like it. But I know You. Help me to learn this new way of resting on You."

A bitter, accusatory, "Why me?" is a useless question which could easily be countered with, "Why not you? Why should you of all the world be exempt from pain?"

But "Why? What's the purpose? What do You have for me, my family, my friends in this? What are we to learn?" That's different. That's healthy. That's good.

Chuck and I had our first introduction to unavoidable illness just after our third wedding anniversary. I went to the doctor because I thought I was pregnant. Instead of carrying a baby, I was carrying what was first thought to be an ovarian cyst that threw my monthly cycle off. What I actually had was a cyst in my abdomen resting against the outer wall of my uterus. It was surgically removed and the tests on it during the operation showed nothing unusual.

It was two days later that my doctor had to tell me that further lab studies indicated that some of the cells in the cyst were malignant. There was no way of determining if any interior damage had been done where the cyst had rested.

Also as a result of the surgery they discovered I had a disease called endometriosis, a condition in which the specialized tissue of the uterus wraps itself around the ovaries and prevents ovulation. As a result a pregnancy is impossible. The only known cure is a pregnancy. (How's that for irony?) The doctor told me a pregnancy could be simulated courtesy of birth control pills, and that conception might still be possible in spite of the endometriosis.

But there was still the mixed cyst. Had it done any damage? Slides of the cyst were sent to Mayo Clinic for another opinion. I was a case study at the monthly seminar of the local Gyn-Ob men.

Advice was mixed. Mayo Clinic and my doctor recommended a hysterectomy as a precaution against a possible cancer. The Gyn-Ob panel recommended I wait and see what happens and in the meantime try to get pregnant.

Chuck and I had to decide. I spent my twenty-sixth birthday weighing the pros and cons.

We decided on the surgery, preferring a definitely healthy me to a barely possible pregnancy and a possible cancer. We've never regretted the decision even though the uterus, studied upon removal, was clean. Without the operation we would never have known for certain that I was not infected. The knowing was so important.

I remember feeling somewhat angry and puzzled at the time. "Lord, wouldn't Chuck and I have produced a child worth making? Don't we have qualities worth combining into a person? Other women have kids. Why not me?"

But countering the anger was the knowledge that God had a

special plan for our lives together and my life individually. For some reason the bearing of children didn't fit into it. I—we—had to learn to accept that fact without rancor. *All* things work together for good.

"I do believe that, Father. Just help me now that it's hard, now that I have to put theory into practice. And I praise You that You are there through it all."

The terrible medical tragedies that face us—and many suffer far, far worse than we did—can be so overwhelming. We either drown in the sea of conflicting emotions that the tragedies produce or we mature into the strong, tried-by-fire saints that God intends for us to become.

Our Lord certainly suffered physically. Some days as He looks down on us as we go our independent ways ignoring Him, I think it must be only His holy love that keeps Him from shouting, "Why did I go through all that, God, my Father? They don't even care!"

He suffered and we care little. We suffer and He cares infinitely.

II

She senses that her gain is good;
Her lamp does not go out at night.

There must be a wonderful sense of satisfaction in starting a business and watching it grow. I've often read in the women's magazines about someone who has developed a hobby, be it Christmas decorations or baking cakes or whatever, into a full-fledged enterprise. I can imagine the joy she experiences in knowing that others consider her product worthwhile.

Our lady in Proverbs knew that gratification. She saw her business ventures bring her gain.

I wish I could say I knew this particular satisfaction from personal experience, but I can't, at least not yet. As I collect my rejection slips month after month, I look with longing toward the day when someone besides Mom will think my stuff worthwhile, when someone besides my closest friends will go out of their way to read something I've written. As I pen this, I have just finished filing with the national government for tax purposes on a taxable income last year of $67.00.

If I felt that my only criteria of self-worth or gain was the measure of success I'd achieved, I'd be in a state of depression. If my self-esteem was dependent on the proportion of acceptance letters to rejection slips, I'd be a loser.

But this type of achievement isn't my touchstone. I don't measure my worth by something as fleeting and temporal as business success or money. I have discovered a sounder foundation on which to build my life.

"Are not two sparrows sold for two cents?" said Jesus. "And yet not one of them is forgotten before God. Indeed the very hairs on your head are all numbered. Do not fear; you are of more value than many sparrows" (Luke 12:6, 7).

I have no idea how many hairs are on my head. Even if I knew now, the next time I brushed my hair, the figure would be obsolete. But God knows and keeps updated totals. If he cares to know something that minute about me, how He must love me!

This love of God, this intense concern and interest He has in me, is my gauge of self-worth. The world may be out to defeat me, but with His love and care as a buffer, I'll be all right.

This great, enveloping love is so clearly stated by Jesus in His prayer in John 17. He is talking with His Father, discussing us, His earthly children. "As Thou, Father . . . didst love them, even as Thou didst love Me" (v. 21-23).

God loves us as He loves Jesus, His only unique Son! How can we ever disparage ourselves when God holds us so dear.

Whenever he's mad at himself, one of my sons has the habit of saying, "I don't like me."

It angers me to hear him say this. I love him, and as his mother, I see a lot of potential in him. When he flays himself in this manner, he's criticizing someone I love, and I don't like it.

Don't you think that it must sadden the heart of God when we go around putting ourselves down? Oh, we may not say out loud that we dislike ourselves, that we know we're incapable, talentless, and dumb. But we think it, and what we think is what we are.

Belittling ourselves is a slap in God's face. He made us as we are. Granted, because of sin there is much room for improvement. What I mean is that God gave each of us the physical appearance, the intelligence, and the talents we have. And who says that any one talent is more worthwhile than another one?

Being unwilling to accept ourselves honestly, being unwilling to accept our abilities and limitations as God's design for us, is wrong. It warps our perspective, lessens our scope of service, and smacks of rebellion against the Father we say we love.

Don't commit the sin of underrating yourself. God loves you as He loves Jesus. Hold onto that thought. Wrap yourself in its security. Never let it pass from your mind.

"Her candle goeth not out by night." (KJV)

"My candle burns at both ends;
It will not last the night;

But ah, my foes, and oh, my friends—
It gives a lovely light."

Edna St. Vincent Millay

As I thought on the second phrase of Proverbs 31:18, I couldn't help but compare it with Edna Millay's famous lines from *A Few Figs from Thistles* and marvel at the different intent of the two women who originated these thoughts.

Edna Millay's fluid, verbal grace is far superior to that of the Proverbs phrase, but the wisdom is in the words of the king's mother.

To some, it may seem fun, daring, exciting to burn one's candle at both ends, to live to and beyond mere physical endurance. Rebelling against moderation and order may, to some, seem needful and desirable, even if the experience is short-lived. The exultation and fascination of the defiance make its brevity acceptable. After all, devotion to burning oneself out is infinitely preferable to no commitment at all.

Then there is the antithesis, the Biblical call to moderation and balance, the wise use of time and talent, so that the candle won't flicker and dim prematurely.

This life of balance may appear stodgy and dull by comparison, and existence devoid of ideas, experiences, and stimulation. How untrue. Where but in the presence of God, the Author and Creator of all realities and knowledge, could there be so great a realization of potential. We, not He, have made His presence narrow and restrictive.

The candle of life that we prize so dearly deserves careful handling. It will burn itself out in God's time, but until that unknown hour, the creative keeping of it is our responsibility.

12

She stretches out her hands to the distaff, And her hands grasp the spindle.

Everytime I think of our woman spinning, a series of pictures flash through my mind.

First I see a calm, homey picture of our lady with her maidens gathered about her working. Since this Scripture passage was written in a time well before spinning wheels, the lady and her maids spent hours together.

This spinning was the tedious process of making thread from the fibers of plants or animals. The process began with the fibers being wrapped about a stick called the distaff. The fibers were pulled off the distaff a few at a time. They moved through the woman's fingers where they rolled together into one continuous thread. Finally the thread was wound on the turning spindle, a smooth stick which was rotated by rolling it against the hip.

In my mental picture, I see the quick, supple fingers of our woman rolling the fibers, twisting them to a consistent thickness. That took talent and practice. Slowly the spindle was filled with thread. Eventually there was enough to weave a piece of material from which a garment could be cut. As I watched, I became aware of the amount of time that went into the preparation of a single piece of clothing. I realized the degree of commitment for something as elementary as a robe. Keeping a family clothed was a massive undertaking.

Now picture two clicks into place, and I focus on the long-term projects in my own life. I don't have to spin, thankfully, but I do have many time-filling, persistent things to do.

The first one I think of is my children. Talk about a demanding, time-consuming, energy-draining job! I've spent only eight years on this project so far, and many more are ahead if I want these boys to grow up into the men they should be.

And there is my church. We began four years ago with seventeen people. We've grown, expanded, developed, but there is a tremendous amount more to accomplish. Visions of a multifaceted ministry reaching all levels of the community will take years to fulfill.

And there are friendships. It takes years to nurture a warm, trusting relationship with a person. Thoughtful considerations and a listening ear are only two of the many working tools for this project.

And of course there is my marriage. (Chuck isn't really at the bottom of my list. I just saved the best until last.) Here is the most demanding of all my chores. The kids take work, but fifteen years hence, I will have completed all I can do in that area. The church is vital to the work of Christ, but others help me share this responsibility. Friends are wonderful, and I love them, but I don't live with them. Clearly my marriage is my most demanding (and enjoyable) project.

The last mental image that the spinning lady brings to mind—unexpectedly—is a montage of faces, people who helped to weave the fabric of my life. I'm surprised at some of the people before me. They are not dear friends. In fact, most of them are people whose lives just brushed mine. They are important to me because they said or did something that struck me at a specific moment in time.

There's Mrs. Williams at a Good News Club. I was nine years old the day she asked all those who prayed more than "Now I Lay Me" at night to raise their hands. I raised mine knowing that I was lying. I was so conscience-stricken that I vowed never to lie again and always to pray meaningfully. I'm still working at keeping both vows.

Then there was the time I was a very awkward fourteen unsure of myself, aware only of my pimples and lack of poise. I'd worked all Sunday afternoon to get my hair just right for the evening youth meeting. I'd parted my bangs and pinned them into what I thought were beautiful flowing waves. After the youth meeting, which I'd enjoyed shored up by my new mental image of myself, I was at the drinking fountain with the other kids.

"Hey," said Dick to me, "your new hairdo makes you look like a horse."

So much for glamor and self-confidence. I learned the futility of trying to impress men.

I remember Mrs. Abel as the first person who ever came up to me and said, "I'm praying for you, Gayle." I was sixteen and I recall being pleased, surprised, and uncertain how to respond. It meant a great deal to know that someone outside my family cared that much about me.

And there was Jim, the first male who told me I was pretty. At eighteen, I definitely felt it was about time.

I remember Mrs. Gordon telling me that the main ingredient an author needed was self-discipline. What was the blow to me wasn't the statement itself but the subtle inference that she didn't think that I had that quality. I determined to show her I did, and I've been grateful to her ever since.

There are others, of course, and they all affected me in some way. They spoke a careless word that wounded all out of proportion or a caring word that encouraged and assured. What is most interesting to me is the depth of the impact of these words in comparison to the shallowness of the relationship.

How do I affect the people I touch briefly? I pray I will weave positive, strong, helpful threads into the tapestry of their lives.

13

She extends her hand to the poor;
And she stretches out her hands to the needy.

Did you ever wonder why you were fortunate to be born not only in America but also in our era of time? The opportunities that await us simply because of the time and place of our birth are mind-boggling. A slight change in God's plan, and I might have been born in Bangladesh, remained ignorant, and perhaps died of starvation. Or I might have been born a hundred or thousand years ago and died when I had cancer.

Why here? Why now? I don't know, but I'm certainly thankful. God has blessed me greatly.

There are some who seem to feel guilty because they were born in a land of plenty. It's a waste of energy to indulge in such an emotion for such a reason. Where and when one is born is beyond his control. But if guilt is foolish, caring and concern are not. The people who are less fortunate need help, and we should be willing to give it.

Jesus' earthly ministry is liberally sprinkled with His literal, physical care of many. Granted, He used His miracles as a proof of His uniqueness, but it's interesting to notice that they were practical things that He did. No whipping up puffs of magic smoke or cutting ladies in half. He realized that men with physical needs must have these needs met before their minds could grasp the spiritual truths He taught. So Jesus healed bodies. He fed thousands. He raised the dead.

We Christians must remember this principle. Feeding the hungry, helping the drunk and drugged, housing the underprivileged, and all such projects are our responsibility.

Don't make the mistake of thinking that all caring for the

physical infirmities of people is strictly social Gospel. It's not—unless that's all we do. Rather, we are to follow Christ's example of caring for physical needs as a means of gaining the people's confidence. We are earning the right to present the Gospel. We know He's the Way. We know He's the Best. But why should others believe what we say? Only because our lives and concern prove it.

Real concern means a lot more than the token Thanksgiving and Christmas baskets. The world is starving its way to Hell all year while we enjoy plenty. Teens are shooting and drinking themselves to oblivion while we are appalled. Gang warfare in the slums makes headlines while we are thanking God for suburbia.

Our lady of Proverbs stretched out her hand to the poor and needy. The idea is not just tossing a few coins, but grasping the helpless and lifting them. It's bending down, reaching out and touching, and pulling aloft.

There are many agencies that help the starving of the world. If you, like me, want to be certain that your money honors the Lord, choose one of the fine Christian agencies and send them a few dollars a month. Right now I'm looking at an ad for World Vision International (Box O, Pasadena, CA 91109). For a very small sum one can support an orphan under the care of this organization. Perhaps if your family had one meatless night a week, that would make available the funds to feed such a child for a month. Think of the wonderful example this would be to your children of the practicality of Christianity.

Of course one of the best ways we can help the world is to sponsor capable missionaries. Any effective church will have a good missionary program. Be familiar with the people you sponsor. Pray specifically for them. Give to their support. Get to know them when they are on furlough. Have them in your home. You'll find they are not the least bit scary. They are, in fact, some of the most interesting people you'll ever meet.

The inner city is one of the neediest mission fields of today. Drugs, alcohol, and violent death stalk the streets relentlessly. Only Christ has the power to free people trapped by these terrible surroundings.

There are always programs for helping in every big city, and quite often a Christian can work effectively through them. We've been involved with one in New York called Fresh Air Fund. The object is to get the poor kids of the city into the fresh air of the suburbs and country. So for a couple of weeks each summer we have a city child live with us. It's beneficial all around. My kids are learning that they've been blessed in a way that no amount of lecturing could ever accomplish. Our guests learn that all men don't disappear or get drunk or rape to prove their manhood, that fathers play with their kids and hold a steady job, that mothers can love and be gentle, and that siblings aren't just rivals. Most important to us, these kids learn that Christ is more than a swear word.

One of our Fresh Air kids, a thirteen-year-old named John, was in church with us one Sunday when the pastor preached on the lack of prayer in our lives.

"I want to tell you something," John said to the pastor after the service. "You don't know what you're talking about. Those Ropers pray in the morning, at lunch, at dinner, and in the evening. All they ever do is pray!"

Thank God he learned about prayer from us.

If you can't have a kid in your home for a couple of weeks, maybe you can send one to a Christian camp for a while. A noted black evangelist near us has an excellent camp for inner city kids. He, and there are many like him, is always in need of scholarship money to finance the program.

If you have the heart to help, you can.

Helping the community in which you live through extra-church programs is a good testimony. Even something like collecting for the Heart Fund is showing Christian love if you do it as unto Him. So is driving the elderly and blind to the doctor's office. So is driving for at a Meals-on-Wheels program. So is going to an old folks home and playing checkers. So is visiting a friend who is housebound due to a difficult pregnancy. So is sharing good Christian books with your neighbors. So is bringing a friend's kids over to your place for the day so that she can relax. So is sending in a meal to a sick family. So is writing a letter to a lonely friend. So is serving on the PTA.

Obviously none of us can do everything. We must pick and choose the services that fit our lives. The thing is, we must each do something.

"What use is it, my brethren, if a man says he has faith, but he has no works? Can that faith save him? If a brother or sister is without clothing, and in need of daily food, and one of you says to them, 'Go in peace, be warmed and be filled,' and yet you did not give them what is necessary for their body, what use is that?" (James 2:14-16).

There are all kinds of needs, some achingly obvious, some subtle, some long-range, some temporary. If we Christians don't care enough for Christ's sake, who will?

14

**She is not afraid of the snow for her household,
For all her household are clothed with scarlet.**

As I read this verse, I am struck with a very incongruous thought. Our mature, fashionable, well-organized lady would have made a good Boy Scout. Not that I see her taking up her backpack and tramping through the woods to some secluded camporee. Rather, I see her as the ultimate in following the Scout motto, which is, of course, *Be Prepared.*

When the cold winds blew, her family had warm clothes. Considering the fact that their home heating units consisted of chafing dish-type warmers, they needed their heavy scarlet cloaks and robes. I sit in my ecologically acceptable 68-degree office and shiver. I don't know what I would have done back then.

This concept of being prepared is vital. There are so many important issues we Christian women must be able to deal with.

Consider our kids.

A woman about to have a baby, especially her first, reads all she can about the impending event. She becomes conversant on all aspects of her pregnancy, and she knows what to expect from her baby for the first months of life. But if she's smart, she doesn't stop there. She continues reading and listens to men and women qualified to give advice on child-rearing. She thinks about how to approach the problems of disciplining a two- or eight- or fifteen-year-old well before the child reaches that age. She is prepared. No last-minute panic and its accompanying bumbles will catch her.

James Dobson, Hiam Ginott, Lee Salk, Bill Gothard, Howard Hendricks—all are read, digested, considered, and weighed against Scriptural principles. Friends are observed. Those who seem to be achieving positive results are analyzed. What are they doing right? How can she fit their methods into her home? She talks with people about raising children, discussing basic philosophies of child-training. She decides where discipline fits in. She learns to distinguish weak parental love that allows too much freedom from strong parental love that chastens and corrects when needed, however painful.

While her kids are five, six, or seven, she learns how to teach them the facts of sex. While they are eleven and twelve, she reads about teen problems and decides with her husband the basic house policies on issues like dating, driving, and curfews.

In a word, she *plans*, so she won't get caught with the slip of her ignorance showing. She understands that even with all her reading, thought, and prayer that events will still trip her sometimes. She also knows that a little preparation can make the embarrassment and pain a lot less frequent.

Another area where we women should do some advance cogitation is death. Men as a whole are consistent in one thing. They die earlier than women. Because of this, chances are most of us will be widows. Thanks to cars, coronaries, and cancer, we don't know when.

Be prepared.

Study the Bible. Learn about "absent from the body; at home with the Lord." Then read books by those who have faced being left behind and through God's strength learned to cope.

A must is *The View from the Hearse: A Christian view of death* by Joe Bayly (David C. Cook). Mr. Bayly lost three sons, one as an infant, one as a child, and one as a young man. He speaks with authority and understanding on the pain of separation and the sufficiency of God's keeping. Also highly recommended is Gladys Kooiman's *When Death Takes a Father* (Baker Book House). Left with eight kids after her husband's death, Mrs. Kooiman conquered through the grace of God the various sloughs of despond that awaited her: loneliness, money problems, the raising of the kids. Then there's Joyce Landorf's excellent *Mourning Song* (Revell) for all of us who must face the slow coming of death.

A short while ago a friend of mine was conducting a Bible study. While the subject under discussion was death, at least one-third of the women dropped out. They weren't comfortable with the topic. How foolish. Death must be faced, grappled with, and defeated. Christ did His part. We must do ours by being prepared so that when we face death, we can cope with it.

I realize that intellectual preparation still doesn't insulate against the emotional reality of permanent loss, but at least there's bedrock beneath to support our saddened feet.

One other area in which we must be prepared is doctrine. "But sanctify Christ as Lord in your hearts, always being ready to make a defense to every one who asks you to give an account for the hope that is in you, yet with gentleness and reverence" (I Peter 3:15).

When you are in a group of people and someone questions an accepted tenet of Christianity, do you feel personally under attack? Do your hands get clammy, your stomach queasy? Does your mind go blank?

Natural reactions. However, it's important to know whether your mind goes blank due to nerves or due to lack of knowledge. If it's nerves, the paralysis will wear off and you can share some thoughts out of the vast reservoir of information you've accumulated through the years.

It's vital today to be able to defend what you believe. Just accepting blindly that the Bible is God's Word or that Jesus is divine isn't enough. It may supply you with a faith of sorts, but it'll never be powerful enough to help you answer the questions that people will quite honestly ask you.

Why did God set life on earth in motion if He knew beforehand that man would sin?

How can a loving God send anyone to Hell?

Why must Jesus be divine? How do we know that He is?

Can I be intellectually honest and still accept Creation?

These are examples of the legitimate questions we Christian women should be able to respond to intelligently. Don't be afraid. You won't find anything to disprove the Bible. It's God's book. You just need to learn to counter seemingly good arguments.

Begin preparing yourself by reading Clark Pinnock's *Set Forth Your Case* (Moody) or Paul Little's *Know What You Believe* (Scripture Press). For a more in-depth study, investigate *Evidence That Demands a Verdict* by Josh McDowell (Campus

Crusade for Christ). For an exercise in erudition, read Francis A. Schaeffer's trilogy, *The God Who Is There*, *Escape From Reason* (both Inter-Varsity Press), and *He Is There And He Is Not Silent* (Tyndale House).

There's nothing better for our faith than a quick course in apologetics or defense of doctrine.

Remember the lady in Proverbs and be prepared. You never know when the snow will fall.

15

She makes coverings for herself;
Her clothing is fine linen and purple.

". . . Make it your ambition to lead a quiet life and attend to your own business and *work with your hands,* just as we commanded you" (II Thess. 4:11).

In today's industrial, assembly-line business world, often the money-making position a person holds is not really satisfying creatively. It may be repetitious in nature, done by rote, or it may be just a piece of the total job so that the pleasure of creating a whole is missing. For this reason it is all the more important for us to have creative hobbies in which we use our hands. It needn't be needlework or sewing like our talented lady of Proverbs. It can be sculpting, cooking, woodworking, gardening, piano playing, electronics, or anything else that appeals to our fancy. All that's required for a hobby to be a restorative is the use of the hands and the involvement of one's imagination.

We are fashioned in the image of a Creator; therefore we are creative. Whether it is the making of a loaf of bread from scratch or the production of a film that tells a story matters not. What matters is the use of our hands in labor that is satisfying.

I find great satisfaction in needlework projects. As I sit here at my desk, I see the bookend covered with flowers I worked in crewel, all red and yellow and green. In the living room are pillows I've hooked. On the wall are my crewel pictures. My closet contains a number of clothes I've made.

Of course, not all my projects turn out as I'd like. I remember the first sweater I knitted. I was in college, newly involved with Chuck. I wanted him to be duly impressed with my cleverness, so I decided to make him the lucky recipient of my first knitting project. I knitted for hours, green fronts, backs, and sleeves growing from the tumbling balls of fuzzy yarn. I was so proud of my finished product. I knew Chuck would be overwhelmed by my skill. I gave him the sweater during a visit at his home, and he tried it on with his family as a suitably impressed audience. He adjusted the sweater, and before my horrified eyes, everyone dissolved in laughter. There were no underarms in my masterpiece. The arms sort of ended at the elbow and billowed to the waist like a huge, green, fuzzy cape.

"A bat," giggled somebody whose identity I have blocked from my consciousness.

Chuck began to flap his arms.

"A bird," gasped someone else in a laugh-strangled voice.

All the while I tried to act sophisticated and untroubled. Now I give gifts in private.

"Her clothing is fine linen and purple."

Our home here in Coatesville is located at the southern end of what is commonly called Dutch Country. Three miles up the road is the first of many Amish farms with their accompanying buggies and mule-drawn plows and curtainless windows and lanterns for light.

The Amish are a very interesting people. One of their obvious characteristics is their manner of dress. The men wear beards, black suits, and wide-brimmed black hats. The women wear long, plain dresses, loosely fitted and covered by long aprons. They also wear their hair pulled straight back in a bun with a prayer bonnet covering it. Heavy black stockings cover what little leg is visible.

The reason for this mode of dress is that they don't want to draw attention to their physical selves. Colorful prints, varying dress styles, and jewelry or ornamentation are considered worldly, detracting from the inner beauty of the individual and coming between the individual and his quest for salvation.

Looking on from the outside, I see that the Amish have chosen one time in history—the 1690s when they were established—as their base year, and they have changed as little as possible since that time. They dress much as people did then and live much as people did then.

Most of us feel this strict enforcement of such a code is extreme and unnecessary. I think, however, that some of us modern Christians have done a similar thing. We have chosen as our base year 1940 or 1955 or 1965 and said that everyone's attire must fit into the style of that era.

I know of a fine church that has a sign in its lobby reading "Pants suits not appreciated." I keep wondering what this sign does to a woman who gets all dressed up in her best—which happens to be a pants suit—and comes to church seeking help. At the very least she'll feel terribly embarrassed at being dressed unacceptably. Or she'll be offended and stay home next Sunday. Or, perhaps worst of all, she'll mistake Christianity for a rigid code of dress and behavior.

"Likewise, I want women to adorn themselves with proper clothing, modestly and discreetly, not with braided hair and gold or pearls or costly garments; but rather by means of good works, as befits women making a claim to godliness" (I Tim. 2:9, 10).

Paul's standard of dress for us women is modesty and discreetness. By this standard, plunging necklines, bikinis, and the braless look are unacceptable in church or out. But a pants outfit can be quite modest and discreet, especially in light of some dress lengths. A pants outfit of taste does not draw unseemly attention to the wearer. Biblically, then, I can't see any support for a stand here, unless, of course you are willing, as are my Amish friends, to do away with all gold or pearls or jewelry or costly garments.

"And let not your adornment be external only—braiding the hair, and wearing gold jewelry, and putting on dresses; but let it be the hidden person of the heart" (I Peter 3:3, 4).

16

Her husband is known in the gates,
When he sits among the elders of the land.

In Biblical times, the gate of a city was a place of much activity. Here the elders of the city met; and matters of law and politics were considered, discussed, and ruled on. Our lady's husband was involved in these procedures and had even gained a good reputation for himself.

This is not to say that all men must be politicians or law-makers. Some will be research engineers like my Chuck. Some will be teachers like my father and brothers. Some will be carpenters and college presidents like my grandfathers. Some will be businessmen like my father-in-law and brother-in-law. Some will be ministers like my other brother-in-law. The list of possibilities is endless. It's not so much a matter of what a man does as it is *how* he does it. And a large part of any man's achieving is his wife.

Certainly some men achieve in spite of their wives. Abraham Lincoln comes to mind. But what might these men have achieved with the support of a cheerful, intelligent, positive woman behind and beside them. "An excellent wife is the crown of her husband, But she who shames him is rottenness in his bones" (Prov. 12:4).

According to Chuck, there is one major characteristic of the wife who is NOT the asset her husband deserves. He claims he's speaking for men in toto when he says that slovenliness or sloppiness is the great undoing of many women.

It must be very deflating for a man to see his woman go from a lovely, well groomed, shapely fiancée to a lazy, overweight, unkempt wife within a few years' time. Not that a man should demand physical perfection. Not that he should expect full makeup and flowing skirts every evening. But he does deserve personal neatness and cleanliness from his wife.

A man has an eye for beauty just as we women do. As a result he will react to us visually. If we are always, or nearly always, an affront to his esthetic sense, he may well look other places for loveliness. His sin, whether in thought or deed, will be our fault, at least in part.

Keep your hair clean, cut, and attractively set. Keep your clothes in good shape. Don't feel selfish if you spend money on your hair, your wardrobe. You do your family a favor if you look attractive and happy. Don't ever give them reason to be ashamed of you.

There are women who look beautiful until they open their mouths. Then with the tone of their voice they ruin the lovely picture they have worked so hard to create. Nowhere is all the inner frustration and tension of a woman more evident than in her tone of voice.

Imagine yourself at the supermarket. You have two little kids with you, kids with curious hands. You have to say to them, "Don't touch that." What would make other women turn and stare aghast and make men thankful that you weren't their wife wouldn't be the words themselves. They are spoken innumerable times and nobody notices. It would be the tone of voice that says those words.

My son Jeff came home from school one day and told me he really liked one of his classmates named Dede.

"You know why? Because her voice is so soft and pretty. It makes me feel good."

I don't know what it is that allows us to become so careless about the way we say things. We allow malice, jealousy, anger, or frustration to make us shrews. We scream at our kids, nag our husbands, make smart, sarcastic remarks about everyone and everything. What a far cry from Paul's urging, "Let your speech be always with grace, seasoned, as it were, with salt" (Col. 4:6).

Mrs. Jones is a Sunday school teacher. She's been teaching the same class for years. She never goes to teacher training classes. She never looks for new and interesting ideas with which to challenge her class. She knows the manual by heart and never researches to enrich it. She just sits and talks Sunday after Sunday, saying nothing.

In short, Mrs. Jones is bored and boring, and her Sunday school class is uninspired and uninspiring.

So is a marriage where the wife is no longer enriching her mind, no longer learning, no longer reaching.

In the past people complained about educating girls because they would grow up only to become wives and stay home to raise babies. Today wise people understand that for anyone, male or female, the acquisition of knowledge is never a waste. The mere possessing of it makes a person richer to himself and to all with whom he has any dealings.

Even after our formal education ceases, our learning doesn't. We either learn to be lazy and let our minds go flaccid, or we learn to expand our world through our intellect.

Talking with Chuck about anything—politics, personal or national economics, church, his job, sports, the family, or the Lord—requires that I be willing to think a little. I'm not an expert in these fields, especially in Chuck's specialty at work, which is ferrous metallurgy, so Chuck can teach me in some areas. I in turn can teach him in others. (Any man of character doesn't mind being taught by a woman.) This constant stimulation of two minds encouraging and teaching each other is one of the greatest pleasures of a good marriage.

"If you seek her [wisdom] as silver, and search for her as for hidden treasures; then you will discern the fear of the Lord, and discover the knowledge of God. For the Lord gives wisdom; from His mouth come knowledge and understanding" (Prov. 2:4-6).

Nothing makes it easier to become spiritually lax than a family underfoot. For some unknown reason, nobody needs you until you sit down, and when you try to pray, the whole world wants to talk with you.

A working mother or a mother with young children is especially pressured to find quiet time for devotional thoughts. Time is such a slippery character that it's difficult to catch enough time to be of value.

Sometimes Jesus found it necessary to rise early and pray before people were about to disturb Him. Maybe you will too.

Sometimes Jesus found it necessary to pray at night after the tensions and burdens of the day were laid aside. Maybe you will too.

In theory a mother at home all day with all her kids in school should have no trouble finding time for her devotional life. Maybe it's the illusion of endless time that's the enemy, but more days pass than most of us choose to count without our taking time for concentrated prayer and Bible reading. I've found that the best time is immediately after the horde leaves for the day, before I get caught up in the million and one things that demand my time.

It's important to establish a pattern for reading your Bible. Select a book and stay with it until you finish it. Underline parts that speak to you. Make notations in the margins of blessings and questions that come to you as you read. If you don't want to mark up your good, leather-bound edition, buy a paperback for your devotional use. Perhaps you are most comfortable using a daily devotional booklet. Fine. Get a good one and use it.

Also establish a pattern for your prayer life. One reason we often miss the blessing of seeing God answer prayer is because quite frankly we forget what we've prayed for. The other major problem afflicting prayer lives is a wandering mind. So I have a written prayer list that I revise monthly. I pray from this list for specific requests for my family, friends, and church. When God answers one of these requests, I check it off. Its exciting to see the checkmarks accumulate.

We make all kinds of noises about wanting God's best in our lives. We want to be the best wives and mothers possible. We want to do well at our jobs. We want to live as Jesus would have us live. Unless we discipline ourselves to read God's Word and talk to Him regularly in prayer, we can't possibly succeed.

17

She makes linen garments and sells them, And supplies belts to the tradesmen.

Have you noticed that our liberated lady here in Proverbs is a working mother? We know she has children because verse 28 tells us they rise up and call her blessed. We know she works because verse 16 describes her purchasing and planting a field. And here we have her dealing with merchants handling her products described.

Our lovely lady, the perfect example we all are to follow, is a working mother? Right, she is. Is that image shattering to you? Can't a mother be a good mother and work?

I decided to check the Bible closely on the issue of working mothers. I found, in a word, nothing.

There are no specific instructions in the Bible addressed to the issue of women being employed outside the home. But before you all rush out and get jobs, let's consider certain Scriptural principles.

Back in Genesis at the time of the Fall, God placed a curse on Adam. "Cursed is the ground because of you; in toil you shall eat of it all the days of your life. . . . By the sweat of your face you shall eat bread till you return to the ground" (Gen. 3:17, 19).

Scriptural Principle One is that a man is to labor. By the sweat of his brow he is to feed himself and his family.

So the man feeds the family while the wife bears the children. Now comes the prospect of training these little people. Whose responsibility is this?

Scriptural Principle Two: It is the mutual responsibility of both parents. The man, as head of the family, is to oversee the fulfillment of this principle, but the actual training is a joint project.

"The rod and reproof give wisdom, but a child who gets his own way brings shame to his *mother*" (Prov. 29:15).

"A *father* tells his sons about Thy faithfulness" (Isa. 38:19).

"As one whom his *mother* comforts, so I will comfort you" (Isa. 66:13).

"For whom the Lord loves He reproves, Even as a *father*, the son in whom he delights" (Prov. 3:12).

"Hear, my son, your *father's* instruction, and do not forsake your *mother's* teaching" (Prov. 1:8).

"Honor your *father* and your *mother*" (Deut. 5:16).

We parents must not overlook our fantastic and frightening responsibility. Once a child is born into our family, the duty to him is there. It comes automatically with the wee one in the fluffy blanket. Before God, we must never forget it.

Traditionally, since the father has been away from home much of the day fulfilling Principle One, much of the work and joy of Principle Two has fallen to the mother. It has seemed a logical arrangement.

For many women it is still a perfectly fine pattern. They enjoy the challenge of running a home and find being a wife and mother an exercise in creativity.

For others with different personalities and desires, the prospect of staying home forever with Junior is like a death sentence. Nothing against Junior, but education, training, and personal drive have created a need for more.

I feel this pressure for personal fulfillment, but because of my career field, I don't face the problem of leaving my home. All I need for my writing is a quiet corner, paper, pencils, and a typewriter. I can write to satisfy myself and still be available to my children.

Many women trained in the art fields can do something similar. They can paint at home, or design and sew at home, or write music at home. But what about women trained in the sciences or with talents in other fields? A lab technician can't bring her test tubes home. A doctor or nurse can't have a hospital in the living room. A computer operator can't buy her own computers. A salesclerk can't sell without a store.

Perhaps such women can do as my sister-in-law Chris. Trained as a nurse, Chris has solved her problem of house fever by working part time. Two or three mornings a week she serves as scrub nurse for a doctor. The rest of the time she's home with her husband, her three small kids, her golden retriever, and her Great Dane. She has the best of both worlds. She doesn't work enough to feel guilty about leaving the kids, and she does work enough to feel needed and fulfilled.

Would that all solutions were as easy as Chris's and mine.

Consider with me the major problem in accomplishing Principle Two, the mutual responsibility to the children, if both parents work. What happens to Junior with both Mom and Dad at the office? Who is responsible for him? If a babysitter is hired, she must be the type of woman capable of training him. She will be assuming your God-given responsibilities while you are gone. The same applies to a child care situation. Are the teachers and the course of instruction satisfactory? *In loco parentis.*

(Don't be upset if your mother doesn't jump at the chance to be your daily babysitter. She's done her stint of tot training and wants to be free to come and go as she pleases. She may not choose to be tied down with another woman's child, even if you are the other woman and the child is her grandchild. Be mature enough to realize that if you feel the compulsion to go and do, so does she.)

Many mothers choose to remain at home while their children are small, feeling that their need for self-expression is less basic than the children's need for a mother. These women return to work after the kids are in school. The teacher is the baby sitter, and *in loco parentis* is less a problem.

One of the most difficult things about being a working mother is the constant emotional and physical stress under which she must live. Can a woman be a wife, a mother, a homemaker, an employee, and not pay for it emotionally and physically?

The Bible presents us Christian women with priorities and the responsibility to keep them straight. God-husband-children-home-self—that's the order. If we can keep everything properly organized, we'll save ourselves much heartache and many problems.

What value is there in being a working mother if your children never call you blessed? What value is there in achieving in the business world if your husband leaves you, emotionally or literally?

At base, it's a matter of ordered priorities. If you can live God-husband-children-home-self, and still have time for a full-time job, go to it. If not, take care.

This issue of the working mother has no easy solution. It's a dilemma each family and each woman must face alone. Differing circumstances, personalities, and compulsions must be prayerfully considered. There is only one surety in this whole thorny issue: God has a personal plan for each of us who seek it. "I will instruct you and teach you in the way which you should go; I will counsel you with My eye upon you" (Ps. 32:8).

18

Strength and dignity are her clothing,
And she smiles at the future.

There is the saying that clothes make the man. They also make the woman. They indicate so much about her: her age, her maturity, her income, her taste, her background, her job.

Interestingly enough it's not the clothes that we women take such delight in buying that are the Biblically recommended attire in this instance. Rather strength and dignity are the beautiful, striking apparel of our Proverbs lady. Regardless of our income or circumstances, each of us can learn to robe ourselves in strength and dignity. All we need is a heart actively tuned toward God.

The strength referred to obviously isn't physical stamina. It's that hard-to-define inner steel that gives a woman character regardless of her physical condition. It's the resiliency that allows her to cope with her ever-changing circumstances. It's the determination that shapes her life and the lives of those about her.

Somewhere through the years an ugly rumor has gotten started. It states that men don't like women of character, determination, and strength. They like soft, pliable, and—if you will—wishy-washy women.

Like most rumors, this one is false. Men may not like pushy, aggressive, overly vocal women, but then neither do other women. But character? That's something else again.

Character in no way attacks femininity. It enhances it. A soft, little, nothing woman who won't think for herself is not memorable, womanly, or particularly Christ-like. It's the highly individual woman of grace, charm, and substance who, when she yields herself to the Master Potter for His molding, becomes a lovely lady.

It's vital in today's world that a woman have strength to face the uncertain future, to answer the kids' questions, to deal with the daily mix-ups, to face the major, unexpected calamities of illness or accident. But where does she get this strength? What is the secret of character?

> *Do you not know? Have you not heard? The Everlasting God, the Lord, the creator of the ends of the earth does not become weary or tired. His understanding is inscrutable. He gives strength to the weary, and to him who lacks might He increases power. Though youths grow weary and tired, and vigorous young men stumble badly, yet those who wait for the Lord will gain new strength; they will mount up with wings like eagles, they will run and not get tired, they will walk and not become weary (Isa. 40:28-31).*

This strength of character comes from waiting on the Lord. Constant daily communion with Him gives us the strength to go on with hope.

My friend Mary Alice has four kids, all nice kids who know the Lord. Like most mothers Mary Alice is concerned about them, their grades, their friends, their romances, their closeness to the Lord. The other day she was sitting in her yard pulling dandelions and talking with the Lord. She asked for His help in pulling up the weeds in her own life and the lives of her kids, just as she was doing in her yard.

"Especially the kids, Lord."

"Don't worry about the kids, Mary Alice," the Lord said to her as clearly as if He'd been standing beside her. "Aren't those kids mine? I'll take care of them."

Wait upon the Lord. What if Mary Alice hadn't brought her children to the Lord until a crisis had arisen? Certainly the Lord would have been there, but not with the beautiful, daily strength she's now finding.

"For God has not given us a spirit of timidity, but of *power* and love and discipline" (II Tim. 1:7).

Hand in hand with strength goes dignity or nobleness of manner.

Even we Christian women often find ourselves in sticky situations. Some are our own making and some are created for us by well-meaning friends. It's how we deal with these circumstances that indicates our degree of dignity and maturity.

Sometimes I sing solos at church. I am not a trained soloist but more the make-a-joyful-noise type. I am ambivalent about my singing, enjoying praising the Lord through many of the lovely, creative Christian songs of today, but at the same time fearing greatly that because of my lack of expertise I'll muff the whole thing and put the entire service on an awkward footing. One Sunday my worst fears were realized. I began on the wrong note. To this day, I don't know where the note came from or what note it was. I just know it was awful! After about six horrendous bars, I stopped, turned to the pianist, and asked her to start again. From some inner well (after all, I'd given the song to God before I got up to sing it), the Lord gave me the dignity to carry off a terrible situation and the wisdom not to compulsively apologize to everyone after the service.

We all make mistakes. Dignity helps us through the embarrassment of it. Dignity helps us stand tall when we'd rather run and hide.

As Christians, our sense of dignity is not based on family or personal worth. It is based on our relationship to Christ. We are clothed not only in the righteousness but also the armor of the One who lent unbelievable dignity to the most shameful of circumstances, crucifixion. Because of His presence in our lives, we can stand straight and tall.

She smiles at the future.

When I think of the uncertainties of tomorrow, it doesn't give me much to be happy about: The Mideast, the Far East, famine, unemployment, crime, all manner of ungodly living. I should smile? Yes, I should smile.

"Because He lives, I can face tomorrow;
Because He lives, all fear is gone;
Because I know He holds the future,
And life is worth the living just because He lives."*

74

Humanity may seem to have gone crazy, and I may even be caught in the vortex of the violence, but God is still on His throne. They may kill my body, but my soul is safe in the hands of Him who lives and rules.

This same brand of logical faith applies as I watch my kids growing up in a more than slightly crazy world. I could become obsessed with fear as I consider what they have to contend with unless, like Mary Alice, I leave them to God.

"How sweet to hold our newborn baby
And feel the pride and joy he brings;
But greater still the calm assurance,
This child can face uncertain days because He lives."*

While these unknown catastrophic possibilities may or may not strike me or my family, there is one known quantity in the future: old age. In some ways I think I fear old age more than a cataclysmic upheaval. I may become senile, crippled, bedridden, or some such thing which will force me to be dependent on others or which will cause others to pity me. For an independent person, this dependence on others may well be life's bitterest trial.

Every time I see a new sign of advancing age (I just found crow's feet the other day), I know senescence is inexorably approaching.

But wait! If God is able to guide me at eighteen or twenty-four or thirty-five, surely He's every bit as able at seventy-five or eighty. If God planned that this year I should be thirty-five, He's also planned that in forty years I should be seventy-five. At any given moment in time I am the age He purposed me to be at the moment.

Also, today I know God in ways I didn't at twenty-one or thirty. Each day I keep learning wonderful, new things about Him. Imagine the vistas of learning that wait for me as I continue to grow older. Do I want to rob myself of these fantastic new experiences because of fear?

I'm learning that old age isn't frightening if I give it to Him, if I let Him age me according to His pattern. Even in our youth-oriented culture, if I can accept wrinkles, corns, and backaches

*from "Because He Lives" by William J. Gaither, copyright William J. Gaither, all rights reserved.

as His gradual refining of me for His Heaven, I'll be able to totter along with strength and dignity as He planned.

Because He lives, I can face not only the cataclysmic tomorrows but also the mundane ones that wear down my physical being. I can anticipate the God-given delights that will be mine even in the midst of the deterioration.

19

She opens her mouth in wisdom,
And the teaching of kindness is on her tongue.

How many times we open our mouths and cringe at what comes out. By no possible standard could those syllables be called wisdom.

These lapses are quite involuntary and accidental, and are usually recognized as such. Still they can cause the speaker no end of embarrassment.

Back when I was beginning to date my husband, he came home with me one night for the prerequisite dinner to meet the family. As is normal for these circumstances, we were all quite nervous. Part way through dinner my father, named Chuck, decided that this new boy friend, named Chuck, was the best possibility I'd produced thus far. So did my mother and brothers, one of whom is also named Chuck.

In spite of his pleasant surprise at his daughter's romantic coup, Dad nearly bungled it.

"Here," he said expansively, "have some more potatoes, Bob."

There was a momentary check in all motion as everybody, including the new boy friend Chuck, digested the fact that Dad had just called him Bob after my old, recently departed boy friend.

"Oh," said Dad, embarrassed. "I just thought I'd call you by a different name for a change. We have too many Chucks around here anyway."

We all laughed dutifully, and the awkward moment passed.

That night after my Chuck left, Dad came to me all apologetic. "Do you think I upset him when I called him Bob? And do you think he thought I didn't like him when I said we already had too many Chucks around here? I didn't mean it the way it sounded."

He felt better when I assured him that we all knew exactly what he meant. He also felt better when he learned that Chuck's mother called me Joyce (Chuck's old girl) the first time I ate there.

We all make these faux pas no matter how wise and gracious we are. My Aunt Jackie, the very soul of tact, was thinking only in terms of energy when she said to her guests after a long luncheon, "Here. Have a mint. It'll help you go home faster."

These verbal accidents are not to be construed as lack of wisdom. Rather they are to be recognized as what they are, momentary slips of the tongue.

Wisdom goes much deeper. It is quite a wonderful thing, not to be confused with intellect or education. Wisdom is in a large part common sense, the capacity to see things in their proper perspective. It's the ability to discern between good and evil. It's the knack of seeing beyond a person's actions to his motives.

We all can acquire wisdom. It is a direct gift from God. It's ours for the asking, though we should realize that it doesn't come in one great glob. It's acquired step by step.

"But if any of you lacks wisdom, let him ask of God, who gives to all men generously and without reproach, and it will be given to him" (James 1:5).

We can acquire wisdom no matter how we rate ourselves on the dumbness scale. Solomon, the wisest of men, said, "The fear of the Lord is the beginning of wisdom" (Prov. 9:10). As we make the Lord the focal point of our lives and put the principles of Scripture to work for us, we increase our wisdom. We begin to see things from God's perspective, and if that's not wisdom, I don't know what is.

Solomon saw God come to him one night in a dream (I Kings 3:5ff).

"Ask what you wish Me to give you," God said to him (v. 5).

"So give Thy servant an understanding heart to judge Thy people to discern between good and evil" (v. 9).

"And it was pleasing in the sight of the Lord that Solomon had asked this thing" (v. 10). And God gave it to him.

We have as much right as Solomon to request wisdom. Only

know that with this precious gift comes a great responsibility. We must act on what we now understand.

"The teaching of kindness is on her tongue."

"In her tongue is the law of kindness." (KJV)

As I read the two translations of this phrase, I am struck by the two sides of the coin of kindness they represent.

The "teaching of kindness" has to do with the instruction our woman gives to others. By the words of her mouth, she urges consideration, love, aid, sympathy, and courtesy.

It's like us mothers when we say, "Now, Junior, you know it's not nice to speak that way to your sister. Be kind to her. Be gentle."

Or us wives when we say, "Now, dear, I think you should be a little bit more understanding toward George and Paula. Try to look at it from their point of view."

Or us women when we say, "Uh, girls, I think it's time to change the subject. Criticizing Audrey isn't going to help her or us."

"Words of a wise man's mouth are gracious . . ." (Eccles. 10:12, KJV).

The "law of kindness" on the other hand, has to do with self-imposed restrictions on our woman's own speech.

A law is a regulation by the government or God under which we are required to live. Our lady of Proverbs has put herself under a legal restriction that she speak only in kindness. She has made kindness a law of life.

In Ephesians, Paul puts us under the same law, though he begins by stating it negatively. "Let all bitterness and wrath and anger and clamor and slander be put away from you, along with all malice. And be kind to one another, tenderhearted, forgiving each other, just as God in Christ also has forgiven you" (Eph. 4:31, 32).

When we forget ourselves, and our tongues speak in very un-Christian patterns, we tend to underplay the seriousness of our behavior. But this breaking of the law of kindness is a very grave fault. In God's eyes it is as wrong as murder or adultery. Sin is sin to a holy God. We, not God, are the ones who categorize sins as greater and lesser.

"Let the words of my mouth and the meditation of my heart be acceptable in Thy sight, O Lord, my rock and my redeemer" (Ps. 19:14).

20

She looks well to the ways of her household, And does not eat the bread of idleness.

When I began to teach the seventh grade, I had a mother who was quite upset about her daughter come to me. The girl, a personable, attractive child, was beginning to keep the wrong company.

"What do I do, Mrs. Roper?"

Being young and ignorant and in awe of parental authority myself, I said, "Tell her to stay home. After all, she's only twelve."

"But I can't stand the scenes when I try to be stern. I can't take her tears. I love her too much to hurt her."

I may have been naive about the difficulties of disciplining a seventh grader and imposing parental authority, but even I knew this mother had already lost her daughter.

Looking well to the ways of our households sometimes requires doing unpleasant tasks. It means placing restrictions on our children and seeing that the rules are obeyed, anguish or no anguish.

My friend, Wendy, has a son just turned seventeen, a courteous, pleasant young man. But he had to be taught to be that way: it didn't come automatically. The first few times he went out on his own with his friends, he failed to call home when he found he would be later than expected. It caused a lot of needless distress.

Wendy could have passed it off like many other mothers with, "I never know where my son is. He never tells me. After all, I'm only his mother."

But she didn't. She chose to make an issue of courtesy and

responsibility. It was uncomfortable and unpleasant for awhile, but she looked well to the ways of her household.

A household, according to the dictionary, is a collection of all who live in a house, the family. So it's not cooking, cleaning, and keeping house that are referred to in our Scripture text. Rather, it's watching out for the inhabitants of your home.

When I was growing up, my father often moonlighted by working nights with a band. These nights he wouldn't get home until one or two in the morning. My mother would wait up for him to greet him and fix him his fried egg sandwich. She could have gone to bed, and no one would have blamed her. Instead she chose to look after this special one in her household.

Looking well to them means knowing where each is, who he is with, how he is progressing in school or on the job, what his hopes and dreams are. It means talking to him, listening to him, and helping him live within the defined limits.

It doesn't mean being a servant to the members of the household, jumping every time they call out an order. It doesn't mean dropping everything every time someone calls your name from the back bedroom. It doesn't mean, when you get to the bedroom and find a kid lying comfortably on his bed reading, that you should obey when he says, "I'm hungry, Mom. Get me something to eat." Not even if he should miraculously remember to say please.

Looking after your family means that you let them all know that you love them. You want to talk to them. But you will not let them take advantage of you. You do all of them as well as yourself a disservice if you let them think you'll jump every time they hold up the hoop. Force them to learn to be independent.

Did you ever think that picking up your son's clothes every day of his life produces a sloppy man who brings a potential mountain-molehill problem to his marriage? Looking well to his development would include training him to be neat.

Or did you ever stop to think that insisting that your daughter dress only in clothes of your choice (even though some of her choices are horrendous to your eye) will produce a woman with no taste of her own, a mere replica of you? Looking after her well would mean training her judgment but not stifling it.

I can remember my own little guys at around age four sitting in their room in tears because I gave notice that they were to put on their own shoes and socks.

"I'll tie your laces when you're ready. Come see me in the kitchen."

From the anguish and volume of the tears, you'd have thought I was requiring a terrible thing of them. I was just forcing them to be independent at their level.

Care for them, look after them, love them openly, but don't be their maid servant or marionette maker.

There's one crucial area where we Christian women must especially care about in our families, and that's their spiritual progress. We must make it our business to know where each member of our household is in his relationship to God. This is so we can train them as they need to be trained and so we can pray for them as they need to be prayed for.

This knowledge isn't acquired by question-and-answer sessions or lectures. Simple observation will suffice. Does your teen-ager's Bible gather dust from Sunday to Sunday, or does it sit on his night table with a book mark that seems to move? Does your husband lead your family in prayers—besides grace? Does your six-year-old make glorious pronouncements about being a missionary and saving the whole world when he grows up?

One Sunday some years back, Chuck and I were sitting in church in front of a mother and her five-year-old son. Something in the service apparently spoke to the boy, and during the closing prayer, he said to his mother, "I think I want to ask Jesus into my heart. What should I do?"

Wow, I thought. How wonderful for that mother to be able to lead her own son to the Lord!

There was a long silence.

"Um, dear, well, uh, we'll talk to your father about it later."

In understatement, I was distressed. Here was a Christian mother who couldn't even point her own son to Christ. No "looking well" here.

Meeting the needs of our families requires a lot of planning and thought. Maybe that's why the Lord caused so many of our jobs around the house to be untaxing mentally. While we make beds, fold the wash, and dry dishes, we can prayerfully debate the best methods of meeting each person's needs.

One of the reasons our lady in Proverbs was able to look so well to the ways of her household was that she didn't eat the bread of idleness. In fact, she's so un-idle that it makes me weary to think of her.

There are many traps of laziness waiting to snare us. It's like we're the trellis and the tendrils of a lazy habit bit-by-bit climb up us until we are so entrapped that we can hardly get free.

I think one of the easiest of these snares to fall into is the trap of daytime TV. The hours wasted by Christians watching soap operas is undoubtedly beyond computation.

I know one woman who actually blames soap operas for her divorce. She sat and watched them all day, ignoring her husband, her child, and her house. The people on TV were more real than her own family, their problems seemed more pressing.

Being satisfied to live vicariously through TV when you could be out meeting people, doing things, living firsthand is such a sad waste of a life. Granted firsthand living takes more energy and hurts more, but the joys are so much greater.

The great danger of these soap operas is that the lifestyle they portray is the antithesis of the Christian pattern of life. Consider the following, which is the basic plot of the last couple of years of a sudser, garnered from some friends who watch it.

Alice falls in love with Steve. They plan to marry. Alice discovers that Steve has had an affair with Rachel who just happens to be married to Alice's brother Russ. It's a toss-up who fathered Rachel's baby.

After much mental trauma, true love triumphs and Alice and Steve wed. But Alice catches an innocent Steve in a compromising situation with Rachel. Divorce. Steve woos Alice again. Remarriage.

Meanwhile Russ is shed of Rachel, and she is having a great time running wild, giving everybody grief.

And Alice's older sister Pat is having her problems too. Her husband, John, was Pat's lawyer when Pat was accused of murdering her boyfriend after he talked her into an abortion after he got her pregnant out of wedlock. John got Pat off and married her. Shortlived bliss. John has an accident and is crippled for a couple of whiny years. Recovery. Pat has no children. Anguish. Corrective surgery, twins who grow to be teen-agers in about three years. John has an affair.

Add to all this the various murders, affairs, calumnies, drug and alcohol addictions, and general hanky-panky on the part of the rest of the stablemates.

This is the pattern Christ would have us revel in?

The same total immersion can also happen to an avid reader who lives more for the fantasy of her books than the realities of her life.

Certainly the situations portrayed in the soaps and books occur in real life all too often. But there's a world of difference between handling a personal tragedy or helping a friend cope, and wallowing in the confused web of convoluted emotional entanglements in a sudser.

"Finally, brethren, whatever is true, whatever is honorable, whatever is right, whatever is pure, whatever is of good repute, if there be any excellence and if there be any praise, let your mind dwell on these things" (Phil. 4:8).

21

**Her children rise up and bless her;
Her husband also, and he praises her, saying:
"Many daughters have done nobly,
But you excel them all."**

Wouldn't it be wonderful if each evening our children and husbands came to us with a hug and a kiss and said, "You are wonderful, Mother (Wife). I love you dearly. I thank God for you every day in my prayers."

Then it would be worth it, worth all the piddly, little problems, all the big, life-wrenching ones, worth all the tears, prayers, and conflicts. It would also be unreal.

This business of compliments is a complex one. As soon as we begin to fish for them, they become valueless.

"Do you love me, dear?"

Of course he'll say yes, though somewhat peevishly.

Or "I try to be a good mother. Goodness knows, I try."

"You're wonderful, Mother."

The only thing wrong is the lack of sincerity and spontaneity.

Most of us love compliments. They are proofs that people recognize our value. They are evidences of love, affection, and friendship. Not only do we need them; we deserve them. Everyone should be praised when he deserves it.

My son was next door playing while the parents of the house were dressing for a formal occasion. When Chip saw Verona in her long dress with her hair piled on her head and her jewelry on, he stared. Then he looked her over carefully from her shoes to her head.

"Wow, Mrs. Grady," he said. "You look like a millionaire!"

She says it made her evening.

We should be teaching our families the value of compliments. By our example, those of our household should see praise in action.

When was the last time you complimented your husband on anything—the way he dresses, the way he mows the lawn, the way he puts his socks in the hamper, the way he plays with the kids, the way he returns his daily lunchbag for re-use? Don't count phony, sarcastic compliments.

And your kids. When was the last time you told each of them you were proud of them for something? Or that you loved him? A positive comment when a kid looks good is infinitely more effective than a lecture when he doesn't. Or praise when he achieves at something than criticism when he doesn't.

When you praise your family realistically and sincerely, they will learn to express their appreciation, too. Eventually they'll even compliment you . . . eventually.

Recently I was telling my mother what a wonderful job she did some twenty years ago in telling me about sex. She shared with me how awkward she had felt at the time but how determined she was that she do a good job. No one had ever told her a thing.

For twenty some years I've appreciated her honesty and thoroughness, and I've just now gotten around to telling her. And there are countless other things she has done for me that I appreciate but have never mentioned. With children, the rising up to bless comes slowly and over the years.

Once when he was three, my son Chip was very indignant because my neighbor's kids thought their mother was a better mother than I was. I tried to explain that each kid loved his own mom best.

"But, Mom, you're so much better."

At thirteen I'm sure his analysis will be quite different. (Undoubtedly it'll be because he'll be too young to appreciate a good thing when he sees it.) But by the time he's twenty-three, if I've done my job properly, the praise should be there. It won't come in great gobs, but in occasional, sincere statements.

Our lady in Proverbs had a husband who praised her, too. Obviously, busy as she was with her projects, her work, and her kids, she still made time for her husband, time to nurture the plant of their union. And he, gentleman that he was, told her how much he appreciated her efforts.

One of the greatest difficulties in trying to wring compliments from present-day husbands is that many of them have no concept of how much these nice things mean to us. Many are so preoccupied with business or problems that they honestly just don't think.

I love flowers. Chuck looks on them as an expensive frippery that dies. For years I've tried to convince him that I think they make a wonderful gift. But it's a hard task, not because he doesn't want to get me a gift I like, but because his perspective is so different!

Last Valentine's Day I wrote the following for my weekly newspaper column. Do you identify?

> Do you remember the first Valentine's Day after you were married? If you're married to one of the very rare men who love to remember occasions, it must have been wonderful. I bet you got flowers, candy, maybe even a gift, and dinner out, too.
>
> If you're married to one of the rest of the male population (as are most of us) maybe you got a card. Maybe, if you suggested it and the Christmas bills were paid, you got taken out for dinner. Maybe.
>
> In our case, Chuck has good intentions. He's not anti-holiday. He's not against admitting he still loves me. He's not even against spending the money. What he is is forgetful. The only holiday I can be certain he'll remember is Christmas.
>
> I still recall the blow it was to my morale when I learned Chuck didn't live for the sole purpose of remembering me on holidays, especially my birthday and Valentine's Day. My romantic side said he should rush home to me on those days with flowers, gifts, and assurances that he realized what a treasure he'd married. I don't know why I expected that. My father never remembered either. I can still see Mom being stoic when everyone forgot it was her birthday.
>
> I finally decided to stop being romantic and start being practical. If Chuck didn't realize that my birthday was coming or that next week was Valentine's Day, then I'd tell him.
>
> "Just think, my birthday is next Tuesday."
>
> "Oh, is it time for your birthday again?"
>
> "Well, it's been a year, you know. Tuesday's a nice day, isn't it?"

"Um."

"I don't mind if we wait until the weekend to go out, though."

"You don't? Okay. Why don't you make reservations somewhere?"

So much for romance.

Regardless, I know that while little remembrances are nice, they aren't proofs of love. Proofs come daily in the kindnesses shown, the considerations given, and the sharing of oneself. It's by these constant affirmations that I know I'm loved.

We are loved of God, too. We know this by the daily care He gives us. We know this by the way He gives us new life. We know this by the sharing of His own Son even to the point of death. "For God demonstrates His love toward us, in that while we were yet sinners, Christ died for us" (Rom. 5:8).

Flowers, gifts, words of praise, and dinners out are wonderful. A man should make a real effort to understand their significance to a woman. But a woman must also make a concerted effort not to over-romanticize her expectations.

My friend Joy has a father who remembers every occasion and a husband who forgets them all. One year her husband's first inkling that it was their tenth anniversary came when the florist delivered a large bouquet of congratulatory roses from Joy's father.

Joy has had to learn to accept her husband and gauge his love in other ways. For example, he'll stand up in a praise service in church and publicly thank God for his wife and her wonderful disposition. This is her thanks, not the visual tokens. It may not be as romantic as low lights, soft music, and flowers, but it's his way.

Praise is meant to be received. Yet how many times have you heard someone brusquely brush aside a compliment as just so much flattery, almost a lie. Such behavior is basically rude because it makes the giver feel foolish.

The husband of one of my friends said he was going to stop giving her compliments because she killed all his joy and appreciation by her reaction. Another friend made the mistake of taking back every personal gift her husband gave her because it wasn't exactly what she would have selected. She can't understand why he now gives her such wonders as barbeque grills.

When someone says something nice to you or does something nice for you, just say thank you. Whether you feel worthy of the compliment is beside the point. The one offering it obviously thinks you merit it. Spare him any awkwardness by sparing him flippant responses.

"You look lovely tonight."

"Oh, you don't mean that. You're just saying it."

In effect, you are calling him a liar.

Be careful. A man hurt because a woman has forgotten the law of kindness will be reluctant to place himself in a vulnerable position again.

The psalms are full of compliments offered to God. Psalm 106: 1, 2 is a good example. "Praise the Lord! Oh, give thanks to the Lord for He is good; for His lovingkindness is everlasting. Who can speak of the mighty deeds of the Lord, or can show forth His praise?"

When David lifted his voice in praise to God, how was his tribute received? God had ample reason to say, "Come on, David! Who are you to tell Me how great I am? You have no idea!"

But He didn't. He was gracious. He blessed David and loved him. He showed us by example how to accept praise.

If the infinite God can be this courteous to us lowly mortals, can't we try to be gracious to each other?

The husband in Proverbs compares his wife to "many daughters," telling her she excelled them all. Consider the Jewish culture in which this statement was given. Consider the daughters of Jewish history who may well have been in his mind when he paid his wife this unique compliment. There are Sarah, Rebekah, Rachel, Ruth, Naomi, Hannah, and countless others.

What a tribute to be compared favorably with these great women. What a challenge to live up to them!

Whenever we modern wives begin to feel that we are doing a good job, all things considered, all we have to do is to think about the line of great women of God who preceded us. That will put things in perspective again. To match their standard of excellence requires from us the same thing that led to their greatness—lives dedicated completely to God.

22

**Charm is deceitful and beauty is vain,
But a woman who fears the Lord,
she shall be praised.**

Charm and beauty are two characteristics most women seek. This fact isn't particularly surprising. A woman of charm is pleasant to be with and a delight to know. A woman of beauty is refreshing to watch.

But charm alone doesn't make a woman of value. Charm is the art of being pleasant for the sake of those you are with. When it becomes the means of cajoling others to do things your way, of manipulating your circumstances, it becomes a weapon of deceit.

We've all known people who turned their charm on and off depending on whom they were with. Delightful around company, they are shrewish at home. Cordial to a certain few, they ignored everyone else.

Charm like this is deceitful.

Beauty, outer physical perfection, is vain and empty if that's all there is to a person.

To be lovely to look at is nice, but to be intelligent is nicer still. To be pretty is good, but to be compassionate and concerned is better still. To be beautiful is wonderful, but to be talented is more wonderful.

Physical perfection is so easily lost. If we base our security on our face or figure, we are headed for disaster. Age will get us if disaster doesn't.

On my evening walk around the reservoir, I cross a little bridge. Each night fishermen are there trying their luck.

One evening just as I reached the bridge, a woman caught a little fish. She unhooked him and placed him on the walk beside her. She quickly recast.

When she flicked her rod and line back for her cast, the hook danced inches from my face. She was oblivious to the potential danger to me, and it happened so fast that it was over before I could move away.

As I thanked the Lord for those couple of inches, I thought of how easily my face could have been scarred. I may not be Miss America material, but it's still my face, the only one I'll ever have. What if that hook had gotten me, and I saw myself only in terms of what the mirror reflected?

Beauty is vain and empty, and not enough.

But a woman who fears the Lord is something else again. Her value system is not dependent on herself and her estimation of her own worth. It is not subject to caprice or whim. It's grounded in the unshakable Rock, secure against danger and storm.

The phrase "fears the Lord" is an interesting one. What is meant here isn't a quaking, shivering terror. It's not the pit-of-the-stomach anguish because He's a holy God and you're a sinful man.

Rather to the Christian, *fearing the Lord* means having a real sense of awe toward Him. He is holy, omnipotent, omniscient, preexistent, and . . . the list of marvelous character traits could go on indefinitely. Because He's all these things in their perfect, absolute state, He deserves our amazement, homage, and respect.

It's this very greatness that should prevent us from being casual with God. He and His authority cannot be treated lightly.

The wonderful thing is that in the midst of all this holiness and majesty, which could scare us quite badly, are His equally fantastic attributes of love and forgiveness.

God is harsh in His judgment of sin, but gentle in His treatment of penitent sinners. If this weren't so, we could be frightened. But His love and forgiveness rain down on any of us who confess our sin, washing the sin away.

Sadly some people seem to have real trouble accepting the freedom from guilt that God offers with His forgiveness. Perhaps it's because they don't feel worthy of the freedom and forgiveness after what they did. Well, they aren't worthy. None of us are. But we have forgiveness just the same.

When a person is unwilling to accept the release from guilt that God offers, he is holding to the concept of God, the holy

Judge, condemning the sinner for his sin. But for the Christian this is no longer the role of God. Jesus Christ has blotted away the believer's sins, all sin, each sin, every sin, and God no longer sits in judgment. We are completely free positionally from the penalty and guilt of sin! God is no longer Judge; He is Father.

"There is therefore now no condemnation for those who are in Christ Jesus. For the law of the Spirit of life in Christ Jesus has set you free from the law of sin and of death" (Rom. 8:1).

Of course, while positionally I may be sinless and guiltless before God, practically I am plagued by sin. Every day I do things wrong. Every day I need to ask to be forgiven, not because God has become my Judge again, but because I want to restore fellowship with my Father.

One of the things that causes me to be most in awe of God is this power to free me from guilt. Once I've said I'm sorry for a given sin, I'm forgiven of it. I needn't repeat over and over for weeks at a time my apologies. Once said is enough if I meant what I said. I needn't flail myself mentally with how horrible I am. I am forgiven!

Monks of the early church used to feel that literally beating themselves purged their bodies more completely of their sins. It never did. It never could. Jesus alone could do that.

Modern Christians whip themselves, too. Oh, they may not do it literally, but the results are just as devasting and painful. They hang on to the memory of a past sin and won't let it go. They won't let go of the lie they told or the sex sin they committed or the abuse they voiced.

One evening I met a lovely Christian woman. We had a delightful evening of conversation. Only one thing bothered me. She who had been a Christian for some time felt compelled to tell me that she was pregnant when she got married. She even referred to herself as a harlot.

Why is she telling me this, I wondered. It's not pertinent. It's none of my business. It happened years ago before she was a Christian. Why begin a new acquaintance with the reliving of that painful time?

Because she still felt guilt. Years later, even after accepting Christ as her Savior and with her husband establishing a Christian home, she still considered herself guilty.

God doesn't mean for her to feel that way. He means for her to

93

be free. In His eyes, she is free from the guilt of this sin. It's only in her own eyes that she's not.

Paul certainly had many painful memories after he met Jesus. Think of the deaths that were on his hands! But God took the sin and guilt away. In speaking of the quality of his Christian experience, Paul writes," . . . *forgetting what lies behind* and reaching forward to what lies ahead, I press on toward the goal for the prize of the upward call of God in Christ Jesus" (Phil. 3:13b, 14).

Paul didn't waste time bemoaning what he'd done before he met Jesus. He didn't waste time moping over things that he'd done before his Damascus experience. He put the past with all its sins and mistakes behind him and pressed toward the new experiences God had for him.

If my friend could only know the same freedom concerning her long ago sin. It can never be undone. But it is forgiven! If only she could say the next time it rises to haunt her, "Nope, no more guilt feelings. I won't waste God's time or mine feeling sorry again. I'm reaching ahead!"

One of the greatest devices Satan ever conceived to limit the effectiveness of a Christian was the calling to mind of past sins and the rekindling of a guilty conscience. Beware of this trap.

This is not to say we can do anything we want because there is no guilt. "What shall we say then? Are we to continue in sin that grace might increase? May it never be!" (Rom. 6:1, 2a).

Also, while the burden of guilt for a sin may be removed from our shoulders by a loving Father, we must still deal with the consequences of that sin. God does not interrupt the flow of life to remove the results of our sins. Therefore my friend will have to explain to her son someday why there are only seven months between the dates on the marriage certificate and the birth certificate.

Still what a great gift is this daily release from guilt, what a great freedom from anxiety! How we can praise God for the privilege of knowing Him well enough to rightly fear Him?

23

Give her the product of her hands
And let her works praise her in the gates.

There are some times when the works of our hands seem in conspiracy to embarrass us, not praise us.

Take one product, kids.

I remember going out to eat with my mother, my grandmother, and my brothers many years ago. When we got to the restaurant, there was no table for five available. Instead they offered us one for three and one for two. Since time was essential, Mom accepted.

She, Grandmom, and I sat together, and the boys, then about five and seven, sat behind us. Dinner was progressing quite well and Mom was just beginning to relax when everyone began to laugh. We looked at my brothers like everyone else and cringed.

Those products of Mom's hands were lining their peas up on their knives, lifting the knives high in the air, and rolling the peas down into their mouths. Their aim was abysmal, and peas were dancing madly all over the table and floor as well as their little tonsils.

Mom's only consolation was the hope that everyone realized that certain products take years to develop, and even then there's no guarantee.

It would be comfortable if there was a promise that when you became a Christian, everything you put your hand to—your kids, your home, your good works, yourself—would turn out well. But there isn't.

What there is is God's promise of help in whatever we are doing for whatever product we are making.

In industry whenever a company wants to release a superior

product, that company has a list of specifications that product must meet. It must be so big, so tough, so resilient, or whatever.

When we Christians want to turn out a superior product, we have a list of specifications too. It's the Bible. Here we find all the basic principles for all the things we must do. We're to cleave to our husbands, instruct our children, love one another, and so on.

In industry a company that wants to be certain its specifications are consistently met has within its organization a division called Quality Control. It is the duty of Quality Control to test and retest the product. If it is found to be below specifications, Quality Control sends it back to be corrected and retooled. In the final analysis the reputation of the company rises and falls by how well the employees heed the advice of Quality Control and measure up to the specifications.

We Christians have an inner Quality Control to help us measure up to the standards of our Rule. We have the Holy Spirit. He teaches us, guides us, urges us to avoid evil and pursue good. When we ignore Him, our products are shoddy, second rate, or broken. Our reputation and the reputation of the One we represent suffers.

In industry Quality Control doesn't work only on certain days or when the workers are actively aware of it. As a responsible part of the company structure, it daily checks on one part of the assembly or another.

So it is with the Holy Spirit. He doesn't work only when we feel Him or when we are very aware of Him. He, as part of the Godhead, is stable, unchanging, and everpresent. He isn't tied to our monthly cycles and our anxieties. He's there directing us whether we *feel* Him or not.

In industry Quality Control checks the final product to see if it's the finest the company can produce. After thorough random testing, it puts it's seal of acceptance or rejection on the product itself.

In our Christian lives the Holy Spirit constantly checks to see if we are doing our best. He looks over *each* product we handle, not a mere random sampling of our products, and either approves or disapproves.

Obviously Quality Control permeates every aspect of an organization. So the Spirit should permeate every area of our lives. Only as He does can we be certain of the quality of our products.

Industry commits itself to Quality Control. It depends on that unit to do what management cannot possibly do itself.

We must make a commitment too. Creating products of value and works to bring us praise in the gates is not a matter of wishing or hoping. It's committing and doing. The Holy Spirit will empower us to do things we aren't capable of doing by ourselves.

We all want the products of our hands to honor God. We all want our works to be done in His name. Our Inner Quality Control can see that we achieve our goals.

24

It's a Matter of Balance

Picture a dry sponge, the kind that gets hard and wizened. Imagine putting one corner under the faucet. Water pours into this section, and it comes to life. It expands, becoming soft and pliable.

But the rest of the sponge is still hard and unyielding. It's getting no water. It's parched while the other corner drips with excess.

Imbalance.

Our lives have various corners too. Sometimes we place all our efforts in one area and that area swells with vitality while the rest of life shrivels. We exist for our kids to the exclusion of our husbands. We please our husbands to the negation of ourselves. We help others to the hurt of our family.

Lack of proportion.

Each aspect of our living must be balanced with the others. Being wife must mesh with being mother which must mesh with being me.

Our proverbial woman found her balance. Through her beautiful example, we can begin to find ours.

We are women—different but equal.

We are wives—submissive but powerful.

We are mothers—overwhelmed but ever hopeful.

We are ourselves—bound but free.

We are God's—sinners but forgiven children.

It's all in the balance.